WHAT WE SAY GOES

Chomsky is the author of numerous bestselling political works,
ing *Hegemony or Survival* and *Failed States*. A professor of
tics and philosophy at MIT, he is widely credited with
revolutionized modern linguistics. He lives outside Boston,
chusetts.

Barsamian, director of the award-winning and widely syndicated
ative Radio, is the winner of the Lannan Foundation's 2006
al Freedom Fellowship and the ACLU's Upton Sinclair Award
lependent journalism. Barsamian lives in Boulder, Colorado.

What We Say Goes

Conversations on US Power in a Changing World

Noam Chomsky
Interviews with David Barsamian

PENGUIN BOOKS

PENGUIN BOOKS

Published by the Penguin Group
Penguin Books Ltd, 80 Strand, London WC2R 0RL, England
Penguin Group (USA) Inc., 375 Hudson Street, New York, New York 10014, USA
Penguin Group (Canada), 90 Eglinton Avenue East, Suite 700, Toronto, Ontario, Canada M4P 2Y3
(a division of Pearson Penguin Canada Inc.)
Penguin Ireland, 25 St Stephen's Green, Dublin 2, Ireland (a division of Penguin Books Ltd)
Penguin Group (Australia), 250 Camberwell Road, Camberwell, Victoria 3124, Australia
(a division of Pearson Australia Group Pty Ltd)
Penguin Books India Pvt Ltd, 11 Community Centre, Panchsheel Park, New Delhi – 110 017, India
Penguin Group (NZ), 67 Apollo Drive, Rosedale, North Shore 0632, New Zealand
(a division of Pearson New Zealand Ltd)
Penguin Books (South Africa) (Pty) Ltd, 24 Sturdee Avenue, Rosebank, Johannesburg 2196, South Africa

Penguin Books Ltd, Registered Offices: 80 Strand, London WC2R 0RL, England

www.penguin.com

First published in the United States of America by Metropolitan Books,
Henry Holt and Company 2007
First published in Great Britain in Penguin Books 2007
This edition first published by Hamish Hamilton 2008
Published in Penguin Books 2009

002

Printed in England by Clays Ltd, St Ives plc

ISBN: 978-0-141-03313-6

www.greenpenguin.co.uk

MIX
Paper from
responsible sources
FSC™ C018179

Penguin Books is committed to a sustainable
future for our business, our readers and our planet.
This book is made from Forest Stewardship
Council™ certified paper.

ALWAYS LEARNING   **PEARSON**

CONTENTS

WHAT WE
SAY GOES

CAMBRIDGE, MASSACHUSETTS (FEBRUARY 10, 2006)

James Traub, in the New York Times Magazine, *writes, "Of course, treaties and norms don't restrain the outlaws. The prohibition on territorial aggression enshrined in the UN Charter didn't faze Saddam Hussein when he decided to forcibly annex Kuwait." Then he adds, "When it comes to military force, the United States can, and will, act alone. But diplomacy depends on a united front."*[1]

As Traub knows very well, the United States is a leading outlaw state, totally unconstrained by international law, and it openly says so. What we say goes. The United States invaded Iraq, even though that's a radical violation of the United Nations Charter.

If he knows that, why doesn't he write it in the article?

If he wrote that, then he wouldn't be writing for the *New York Times*. There is a certain discipline that you have to meet. In a well-run society, you don't say things you know. You say things that are required for service to power.

That reminds me of the story of the emperor Alexander and his encounter with a pirate.

I don't know if it happened, but according to the account from Saint Augustine, a pirate was brought to Alexander, who asked him, How dare you molest the seas with your piracy? The pirate answered, How dare you molest the world? I have a small ship, so they call me a pirate. You have a great navy, so they call you an emperor. But you're molesting the whole world. I'm doing almost nothing by comparison.[2] That's the way it works. The emperor is allowed to molest the world, but the pirate is considered a major criminal.

Eighteen Pakistani civilians were killed in a U.S. missile attack on Pakistan in January 2006. The New York Times, *in an editorial, commented, "Those strikes were legitimately aimed at top fugitive leaders of Al Qaeda."[3]*

That's because the *New York Times* agrees, and always has, that the United States should be an outlaw state. That's not surprising. The United States has the right to use violence where it chooses, no matter what happens. If we hit the wrong people, we might say, "Sorry, we hit the wrong people." But there should be no limits on the right of the United States to use force.

The Times *and other liberal media outlets are exercised about domestic surveillance and invasions of privacy. Why doesn't that concern for law extend to the international arena?*

Actually, the media are very concerned, just like James Traub, with violations of international law: when some enemy does it. So the policy is completely consistent. It should never be called a double standard. It's a single standard of subordination to power. Surveillance is bothersome to people in power. They don't like it. Powerful people don't want to have their e-mails read by Big Brother, so, yes, they're kind of annoyed by surveillance. On the other hand, a gross violation of international law—what the Nuremberg Tribunal called "the supreme international crime" that "contains within itself the accumulated evil of the whole"—for example, the invasion of Iraq, that's just fine.[4]

There is an interesting and important book, which naturally has hardly been reviewed, by two international law specialists, Howard Friel and Richard Falk, called *The Record of the Paper*. It happens to focus on the *New York Times* and its attitude toward international law, but only because of the paper's importance.[5] The rest of the press is the same. Falk and Friel point out that the practice has been consistent: if an enemy can be accused of violating international law, it's a huge outrage. But when the United States does something, it's as if it didn't happen. To take one example, they point out that in the seventy editorials on Iraq from September 11, 2001, to March 21, 2003, the invasion of Iraq, the words *UN Charter* and *international law* never appeared.[6] That's typical of a newspaper that believes the United States should be an outlaw state.

Martin Luther King Jr., in his April 4, 1967, Riverside Church speech, said, "Even when pressed by the demands of inner truth, men do not easily assume the task of opposing their government's policy, especially in time of war."[7] Is that true?

You see that anywhere you look. It's obviously true in the United States. But was the United States "at war" in 1967? King suggests it was. It's an odd sense of being at war. The United States was attacking another country—in fact, it was attacking all of Indochina—but had not been attacked by anybody. So what's the war? It was just plain, outright aggression.

Howard Zinn, in his speech "The Problem Is Civil Obedience," says civil disobedience is "not our problem. . . . Our problem is civil obedience," people taking orders and not questioning. How do we confront that?[8]

Howard is quite right. Obedience and subordination to power are the major problem, not just here but everywhere. It's much more important here because the state is so powerful, so it matters more here than in Luxembourg, for example. But it's the same problem.

We have models as to how to confront it. First of all, we have plenty of models from our own history. We also have examples from other parts of the hemisphere. For example, Bolivia and Haiti had democratic elections of a kind that we can't even conceive of in the United States. In Bolivia, were the candidates both rich guys who went to Yale and joined the Skull and Bones Society and ran on much the same program because they're supported by the same corporations? No. The people of Bolivia elected someone from their own ranks, Evo Morales. That's democracy. In Haiti, if Jean-Bertrand Aristide had not been expelled from the Caribbean by the United States in early 2004, it's very likely that he would have won reelection in Haiti. In Haiti and Bolivia, people act in ways that enable them to participate in the democratic system. Here, we don't. That's real obedience. The kind of disobedience that's needed is to re-create a functioning democracy. It's not a very radical idea.

Evo Morales's victory in Bolivia in December 2005 marks the first time an indigenous person has been elected to lead a country in South America.

It's particularly striking in Bolivia because the country has an indigenous majority. And you can be sure that the Pentagon and U.S. civilian planners are deeply concerned. Not only is Latin America falling out of our control, but for the first time the indigenous populations are entering the political arena, in substantial numbers. The indigenous population is also substantial in Peru and Ecuador, which are also big energy producers. Some groups in Latin America are even calling for the establishment of an Indian nation. They want control of their own resources. In fact, some of them don't even want those resources developed. They'd rather have their own lives, not have their society and culture destroyed so that people can sit in traffic jams in New York. All this is a big threat to the United States. And it's democracy, functioning in ways that by now we have agreed not to let happen here.

But we don't have to accept that. There have been plenty of times in the past when popular forces in the United States have caused great change. You mentioned Martin Luther King. He would be the first to tell you that he didn't act alone. He was part of a popular movement that made substantial achievements. King is greatly honored for having opposed racist sheriffs in Alabama. You hear all about that on Martin Luther King Day. But when he turned his attention to the problems of poverty and war, he was condemned. What was he doing when he was assassinated? He was supporting a strike of sanitation workers in Memphis and planning a Poor People's March on Washington. He wasn't praised for that, any more than he was praised for his rather tepid, delayed opposition to the Vietnam War. In fact, he was bitterly criticized.[9]

This isn't quantum physics. There are complexities and details. You have to learn a lot and get the data right, but the basic principles are so transparent, it takes a major effort not to perceive them.

TWO

LEBANON AND THE CRISIS IN THE MIDDLE EAST

CAMBRIDGE, MASSACHUSETTS (AUGUST 15, 2006)

The official story about the Israeli invasion of Lebanon goes like this: Israel acted in self-defense after Hezbollah, in a cross-border attack on July 12, killed eight of its soldiers and captured two others.[1] President Bush said Hezbollah attacked Israel and started the crisis.[2] Are there any holes in the official story?

Quite a lot of holes. The narrow facts are accurate. However, it's necessary to point out that the United States and Israel have no objection whatsoever to the capture of soldiers and even to the much more serious crime of kidnapping civilians. Israel has been abducting civilians for decades, and no one has ever suggested that anyone should invade Israel in response.[3] Just to make it more dramatic, the recent upsurge in violence did not begin on July 12. It began in Gaza after June 25, when Hamas captured an Israeli soldier at the border and also killed two others.[4] That led to a huge upsurge of violence in which about forty Palestinians in Gaza were killed by Israel in June and more than one hundred and seventy were killed from the Israeli escalation of attacks on June 28 through July.[5] Israeli violence more than quadrupled in a month.

But something also happened on June 24, one day earlier, namely, Israeli forces abducted two Palestinian civilians in Gaza, a doctor and his brother.[6] It was known; you can find occasional mentions of it.[7] But nobody reacted. No one suggested that Israel should be invaded and half destroyed. So, by our own standards, there is no justification whatsoever for the U.S.-Israeli attack on Lebanon. That's one point.

Another is that, whatever one thinks of the Hezbollah action, it did have official reasons. One was exchange of prisoners. To go back a couple of months, in February 2006, about 70 percent of the Lebanese population, which doesn't like Hezbollah particularly, were in favor of the capture of Israeli soldiers to exchange with prisoners because they know perfectly well that Israel has been kidnapping and killing civilians in Lebanon for decades.[8] We don't know the exact numbers, it's all kept secret. Hezbollah's other official reason was an expression of solidarity and support for the people of Gaza, who were under bitter attack. In the entire Arab world, Hezbollah provides the only source of meaningful support for the Palestinians today.

However, there is also a very rich background that is barely even discussed. The immediate background is that in January 2006, Palestinians held a free election and they voted the wrong way, electing Hamas to a majority of seats in the parliament.[9] You're not allowed to vote the wrong way in a free election. That's our concept of democracy. Democracy is fine as long as you do what we say, but not if you vote for someone we don't like. So instantly Israel and the United States instituted harsh punishment of the Palestinians, cutting off funds, stepping up atrocities, and starving them, to punish the Palestinians. That pretty much tells you what is meant by "democracy promotion." In particular, Israel stepped up its crimes in Gaza, which were already serious. As Israeli human rights groups point out, Israel has turned Gaza into the biggest prison in the world.[10]

Meanwhile, on the West Bank, Israel, with U.S. backing as always, is carrying out a program that Israel euphemistically calls "convergence" and the United States describes as "withdrawal." In fact, it is a program of annexation and cantonization through which Israel is annexing valuable land and the major resources, particularly water, and designing settlement and infrastructure projects so as to break up the shrinking Palestinian territories into unviable cantons. These are virtually separated from

one another and all virtually separated from whatever
tiny corner of Jerusalem is to be left to Palestinians as the
center of their commercial, educational, and cultural life.[11]
Israel is taking over the Jordan Valley, again with U.S.
backing. So, in addition to the major prison in Gaza, several prisons are being established on the West Bank.

All of these U.S.-backed Israeli programs are, of
course, totally illegal, in violation of UN Security Council
orders, World Court decisions, and so on. And the conditions for Palestinians under occupation are very harsh
and brutal, as they have been for years.

*According to many sources, Hezbollah in Lebanon and
Hamas in Palestine do not recognize Israel and are dedicated
to its eradication. They are also launching Qassam rockets
at Israel from Gaza and Katyusha and other rockets from
Lebanon.*

Let's start with Hamas. Hamas had observed a truce with
Israel for a year and a half that ended only after Israeli
atrocities sharply picked up again. Some Palestinians did
fire Qassam rockets from Gaza, which was criminal and
foolish. But we know the reason. It's a reaction to Israel's
continuing atrocities and its takeover, annexation, and cantonization programs. During the year and a half Hamas
observed a truce, though, Israel refused to accept it and
continued to carry out assassinations, bombings, and of
course its illegal cutoff of funds. Hamas has indicated

repeatedly that it is calling for a long-term, indefinite truce and will enter negotiations on a two-state settlement if Israel commits itself to withdrawing from the occupied territories.

What about Hezbollah? First of all, as far as rockets are concerned, the United Nations keeps very careful records of what happens on the Israel-Lebanon border. The UN has registered hundreds of Israeli border violations, overflights, sonic booms, and other actions on essentially a daily basis, but did not record one confirmed case of a Hezbollah rocket from May 2000, when Israel withdrew from southern Lebanon, up until July 2006, apart from a May 28, 2006, firing in retaliation for Israeli cross-border air strikes, artillery, mortar, and tank fire. Otherwise, there was not a single confirmed case.[12]

Hezbollah's position is that it does not regard Israel as a legitimate state. It doesn't think Israel ought to exist. However, Hassan Nasrallah, its leader, has said repeatedly that Hezbollah will accept whatever the Palestinians accept. If the Palestinians accept a two-state settlement, Hezbollah won't like it, but they will accept it. Incidentally, the Iranian position is exactly the same. The West loves Mahmoud Ahmadinejad's crazed outbursts, but he has a superior who is in charge, the supreme leader of Iran, Ayatollah Ali Khamenei. And Khamenei has declared that Iran accepts the Arab League position: normalization of relations with Israel in a two-state settlement on the international border, in other words, the international consensus.[13] The only two major actors that do not accept this consensus are the United States and Israel. So the right question to ask is: What are we going to do about the fact that the United States and Israel continue to reject and to block a diplomatic settlement of the Israel-Palestine problem, and render it impossible by their illegal actions, as they have for the past thirty years? That's the question we ought to ask.

You met with Nasrallah when you were in Lebanon. What was your take on him?

About the same as everyone else who has met him. For example, the reaction of Edward Peck, who was a high figure in counterterrorism in the Reagan administration, was about the same as mine. Peck said Nasrallah seems reasonable and pragmatic.[14] He's thoughtful and answers the questions you ask him. You can like what he says or not, but you're getting serious answers to serious questions. On Israel, he says what I just repeated. His most controversial position has to do with Hezbollah maintaining weapons.

I spent even more time in Lebanon, which was never reported, with the strongest opponents of Hezbollah. With two friends from here, my wife and I went to meet the Druze leader Walid Jumblatt. We spent quite a few hours talking to him and to Chibli Mallat, the Maronite presidential candidate and constitutionalist, who is also very anti-Hezbollah. I asked them and others in Lebanon how they answered Hezbollah's reasoning about keeping their weapons. Unfortunately, nobody had an answer. And I don't know the answer.

The issue of Hezbollah's weapons goes back to the question: Does Lebanon deserve to have a deterrent to U.S.-Israeli aggression? That's not abstract. The current invasion of Lebanon is the fifth in the last thirty years. Every one has been disruptive and violent. One of them, in 1982, wiped out a large part of the country and killed probably twenty thousand people.[15] This is not a joke. So, do they have a right to a deterrent? If nobody has a right to a deterrent against U.S.-Israeli aggression, the answer is clear: they don't. The United States and Israel are allowed to invade anyone they like. If Lebanon does have a right to a deterrent, what is it? It can't be the Lebanese army, which is much too weak and penetrated by the United States. One credible deterrent would be a U.S. commitment to stop any Israeli invasion. Maybe an asteroid will hit the earth tomorrow, too. That's our problem. If people like you and me and others in the United States cannot provide that deterrent, it doesn't count.

What's the alternative? Hezbollah's argument is that the only thing that deters Israel is guerrilla warfare. Nothing else prevents Israel from occupation. Israel had, after all, occupied Lebanon illegally for twenty-two years, with U.S. support, in violation of Security Council orders.

It was a brutal and oppressive occupation, and only guerrilla war finally drove them out in 2000.

The government of Lebanon is ambivalent about Hezbollah's weapons. The position of Prime Minister Fouad Siniora—who is a Sunni, not pro-Hezbollah, which is Shia—and of the government is that Security Council Resolution 1559, which calls for disarmament of Lebanese militias, does not apply to Hezbollah because it's not a militia but a resistance force. You can agree or not agree with the government of Lebanon, but that argument needs an answer.

It is worth mentioning that polls in Lebanon several months prior to the invasion found that "58 percent of all Lebanese believed Hizbullah had the right to remain armed, and hence, continue its resistance activity."[16] I'm quoting Amal Saad-Ghorayeb, the Lebanese academic, who is a leading specialist on Hezbollah, widely quoted and published in the U.S. mainstream, and by no means pro-Hezbollah. She was also involved in organizing the polls. She points out further that by late July, during the invasion, that figure rose to 87 percent of Lebanese, including 80 percent of Christians and Druze. She concludes:

> Thanks to the high death toll, with close to one-quarter of the population displaced, and the colossal material destruction of the economy wreaked by Israel's war machine, Hizbullah's "logic of resistance" and deterrence has been both vindicated and demonstrated. It has

stepped in to fill the huge political and military vac-
uum left by the state, the resistance's ongoing counter-
attacks paralyzing Israel on the ground. The Lebanese
reject the self-designated role that US and Israeli officials have taken on as spokespersons for the Lebanese,
along with their purported favour of ridding the
Lebanese, once and for all, of Hizbullah. . . . Like their
predecessors in Afghanistan, Iraq, and Palestine, the
Lebanese are starting to equate the US's suffo-
cating desire to bring them "freedom" with the kiss of
death.[17]

Another success of the U.S.-Israel reliance on the
mailed fist.

*You just mentioned UN Security Council Resolution 1559.
Tim Llewellyn, who used to work for the BBC, calls it a
"unique interference by the Security Council in Lebanon's internal affairs."[18] Is it?*

It certainly is unusual, but I don't know whether it's actually unique. The Security Council typically does not intervene in the internal affairs of other countries. One part of
1559 that is not unique is the call for Syrian withdrawal. It
was cynical and hypocritical but within the rights of the
Security Council. In 1976, Syria entered Lebanon with the
support of the United States and Israel. Its task then was
to kill Palestinians, so that was just fine. Syria stayed there

with the backing of the United States. The first Bush administration supported Syria remaining in Lebanon because it wanted to build up a coalition for the Gulf War that would include Arab states. But now, for their own cynical reasons, the United States and France have decided that Syria should withdraw. It's true that Syria should withdraw, but it should have withdrawn in 1976.

The other part of the UN resolution, about the internal affairs of Lebanon, is, as Llewellyn said, dubious. That's not the Security Council's role. It's up to the people of Lebanon to decide how they want to deal with the threat of U.S.-Israeli aggression.

Incidentally, people talk about the "Israeli invasion of Lebanon," but that's not accurate. The jet planes, the missiles, the cluster munitions are made here. And the United States provides them to Israel in massive numbers precisely to permit aggression. So it's a U.S.-Israeli invasion. The United States also vetoed a call for a cease-fire in the United Nations and then blocked a cease-fire for weeks.[19] So the United States has direct participation in this invasion, as in the earlier ones.

Seymour Hersh wrote an article in the New Yorker *called "Watching Lebanon: Washington's Interests in Israel's War." The Bush administration, he asserts, "was closely involved in the planning of Israel's retaliatory attacks."[20] What do you think of Hersh's reporting?*

He's a terrific reporter, and I'm sure he's reporting exactly what was told to him. But his sources are intelligence officials and diplomats, often unnamed. Their task is not to tell people the truth but to tell people what they want them to hear. You've got to understand that any report from an unidentified intelligence or diplomatic source is what they want you to believe. It may or may not be true.

I have no special sources, but I drew pretty much the same conclusions as Hersh, with some modification. For one thing, it cannot be that the United States was involved in the detailed planning of the attack on Lebanon because it took place instantly, within hours of the capture of the Israeli soldiers, in fact. So there was no time for detailed planning. Israel obviously had contingency plans, of course, just as I'm sure there are contingency plans to drive the whole population of the West Bank into Jordan or the Gulf. Every state has contingency plans, but Israel's decision to implement them probably was made in consultation with Washington. Israel saying "Give us a green light and we go ahead," though, is different from the United States planning the attack.

Hersh suggests in his article that one of the goals of the United States was to eliminate a Lebanese deterrent to a U.S. attack on Iran. You can be pretty confident this is true, since a major deterrent to a potential U.S.-Israeli attack on Iran is the possibility of a Hezbollah attack on Israel in reaction. Rightly or wrongly, the United States and Israel thought that they could get rid of that deterrent with a massive air attack on southern Lebanon.

In her book Israel/Palestine, *Tanya Reinhart reviews the record of Ariel Sharon and Ehud Barak on Lebanon. She writes that Sharon hoped to "create a 'new order' in Lebanon. Since that failed, and the Israeli occupation of Southern Lebanon turned out to be more and more costly over the years, Sharon developed a new plan: Israel should withdraw unilaterally from Lebanon"—which it did in May 2000—"thus achieving the world's recognition as the peaceful side." Sharon's strategy was that "Israel should then wait for some incident. Under the new circumstances, even the slightest incident will be viewed as a legitimate reason for Israel to launch a devastating attack against Lebanon and Syria."[21]*

Reinhart is extremely acute. She knows the situation very well and has to be taken seriously.[22] She's an old friend, so take that into account. But I don't think they intend to attack Syria. If they're reasonable—I'm assuming rationality, which I think is a fair assumption in Israel's case, though not necessarily in the case of Dick Cheney and Donald Rumsfeld—I think Israel would be concerned about the nature of the successor regime in Syria. Bashar al-Assad is doing pretty much what Israel wants. He is keeping quiet. He is letting Israel take over—illegally, of course, annexing the Syrian Golan Heights—and not making much of a fuss about it. Syria is very weak as a military force. So from Israel's point of view, the government in Syria is more or less acceptable. A successor regime is likely to be an Islamic fundamentalist one, another Hezbollah, and may turn to guerrilla warfare, which is the last thing Israel wants. So my suspicion is that Israel doesn't want to attack Syria.

A "new order" in Lebanon is an old plan. Even before Israel was established in 1948, there were ideas about setting up a client regime in Lebanon, a Maronite state. It's no secret that the main purpose of the 1982 invasion was to put an end to the embarrassing PLO calls for negotiations and to drive the PLO out of Lebanon. It was described as a war "to defend the Galilee," but in fact it was an invasion to take over the West Bank. A secondary goal was to institute a Maronite client regime in Lebanon. Other Israeli commentators have also reached the same conclusion as Reinhart. Uri Avnery, who is closer to the establishment but nonetheless a critic, has said that the goal of the current invasion is to revitalize Sharon's old plan of installing a Maronite kingdom.[23] That may be. I don't know, but I kind of doubt it. You could imagine Israel getting away with this in 1982—they almost did—but now it's pretty hard to imagine. For one thing, the Maronites are split. One large segment, led by General Michel Aoun, is linked more or less to Hezbollah. In addition, the Maronites have nowhere near the power they had back in 1982, when they had a big armed militia supported by Israel.

The Israeli military has a vaunted reputation for performance in past wars. Siddharth Varadarajan, writing in the Hindu *on August 14, had this comment to make: "More than 30 years of enforcing a military occupation and fighting children and poorly equipped guerrillas have clearly taken their toll on the ability of the legendary Israeli army to fight a full-fledged war."*[24]

I'm not a military expert, but I don't quite agree. I think that if Israel were to have a war with, say, Syria, it wouldn't be a six-day war, it would probably be a fifteen-minute war. I think that's the kind of war Israel can probably still fight, as opposed to a serious guerrilla war. And here Hezbollah is unique. Israel is fighting a guerrilla movement that is deeply entrenched in the population and, from a military point of view, pretty sophisticated. They bombed and bombed, and they didn't get anywhere. Israel didn't want to send in ground troops because Israel knew they would be fighting a guerrilla war, the same kind that drove them out of Lebanon in the first place. And when they went in, they had tough going everywhere. The Hezbollah forces were behind them, in front of them. It was kind of like fighting what the United States called the Viet Cong, the official propaganda term for the National Liberation Front forces in South Vietnam, who were really just the population. Not only is that tough on your own forces, but it's a war against the population, and we know what that means. When they say they're attacking "Hezbollah targets," that means they're attacking civilian society. Take south Beirut, where I was a couple of months ago. It's a poor part of the city and is a "Hezbollah target." Most of the population are Shiites who support Hezbollah or Amal, which is a close ally of Hezbollah, with about the same program, so if you want to attack Hezbollah you have to attack the civilian society.

You can also get fanatics, like Alan Dershowitz, who said that more than 80 percent of Lebanese support the Hezbollah resistance, so therefore all Lebanese are legitimate targets.[25] So if anybody supports resistance to the holy state, they are a legitimate target for destruction. Try to find an analogue for that. I've been thinking, and I haven't been able to find one. So, way out at the hysterical extreme, you get Dershowitz's view. And from there on over, you get to the moderates, who say that the attack on Lebanese civilians is "disproportionate."[26] It's not disproportionate, it's outrageous.

Nobody is pure as the driven snow. But the problem we should be concerned with is the United States. After all, that's us. That's what we're doing.

After the assassination of the former Lebanese prime minister Rafik Hariri on February 14, 2005, there were mass street demonstrations, a so-called Cedar Revolution was encouraged by the United States. Syrian troops left the country. There was going to be a new era in Lebanon.

First of all, after the Cedar Revolution, antagonism toward and suspicion of the United States in Lebanon was even higher than suspicion of Syria. George Bush would like to take credit for the Cedar Revolution, but the Lebanese see it differently. The Cedar Revolution was a Lebanese program. France and the United States for once didn't impede a move toward democracy—again for their own cynical reasons—but that's about the most you can say.

From Washington's perspective, any democracy that emerges has to be one subordinated to U.S. interests. The United States wants Lebanon to become a commercial and financial center run for the wealthy. One of the reasons that Hezbollah became so powerful is that the Lebanese government did essentially nothing for poorer Shiites in south Beirut and south Lebanon. Hezbollah's prestige comes not just from leading the guerrilla forces that drove Israel out of Lebanon in 2000, but from providing social services—health, education, financial aid. For many Lebanese, Hezbollah is the government. As with other Islamic fundamentalist movements, that's the basis for its enormous popular support. You don't want to have nonstate actors, especially military ones, inside a state, but unless the fundamental problems are dealt with, that's going to happen. It's almost inevitable. In fact, the United States and Israel substantially helped create Islamic fundamentalist extremism by destroying secular nationalism. If you destroy secular nationalism, people aren't going to just say, "Okay, cut my throat." They're going to turn somewhere else. And that somewhere else has been extremist religious fanaticism.

In fact, sometimes these movements are actively encouraged. Since the Second World War, the United States has been the world's strongest outside supporter of extremist Islamic fundamentalism. Washington's oldest and most valued ally in the Arab world is Saudi Arabia. Iran looks like a democratic heaven in comparison. The threat to Saudi Arabian religious extremist tyranny was secular nationalism, mainly embodied by Gamal Abdel Nasser. So Nasser became an enemy because he threatened the U.S. base of extremist religious fundamentalism, Saudi Arabia, which happens to control the oil, the underlying reason. In 1967, Israel performed a huge service to the United States, to Saudi Arabia, and the energy corporations by essentially eliminating secular Arab nationalism, which was threatening to use the resources of the region for the needs of its own population. That's intolerable. They're "our" resources, as George Kennan said a long time ago, and we have to "protect" them.[27]

The same thing has happened time after time. Israel created Hamas by destroying the secular Palestine Liberation Organization, which was calling for negotiations and settlement. Since that was the last thing Israel and the United States wanted, they destroyed it. And then what happened? The population didn't disintegrate.

They turned to something else, in this case, religious fundamentalism. The jihadi movement already existed in the 1970s—they were responsible for the assassination of Anwar Sadat in 1981—but was mainly Egyptian-based until the United States gave them a huge shot in the arm by organizing them to fight the Russians in Afghanistan. Not *for* the Afghans—the U.S. mobilization probably prolonged the Russian occupation—but against the Cold War enemy.

In Pakistan, which is now a major center for radical Islamism, the movement began with former president Muhammad Zia ul-Haq, who was strongly supported by the Reagan administration. In fact, all through its tenure, the Reagan administration pretended that Zia wasn't developing nuclear weapons. Of course they knew that he was. But every year they would religiously certify that Pakistan was not developing nuclear weapons because they wanted to support their radical, extremist, fundamentalist friend. They knew perfectly well that Saudi Arabia was funding the extremist madrassas, the religious schools that undermined the Pakistani educational system, which had been pretty good beforehand. People like Pervez Hoodbhoy, a Pakistani nuclear physicist, now deplore that you can't get students to study the sciences because schools teach only the Koran. That wasn't true in the past. All of these developments were supported by the Reagan administration. A number of the same Reagan-era officials are in office again now.

They're ecumenical. Washington will support anyone who accords with U.S. policies. Saddam Hussein happened to be a secular maniac, but they supported him, too. When he invaded Iran, the United States favored that. In fact, they pretty much won the war for him.

What is the relationship among Shiites in Iraq, Iran, and in Lebanon?

You have to give Donald Rumsfeld, Dick Cheney, and Paul Wolfowitz credit. They have created a Shiite-dominated state in Iraq that has close links to Iran and may turn out to be another religious fundamentalist state. They created it—it wasn't there before. Whatever they thought they were doing, that's what they achieved. In fact, the Iraqi parliament passed a resolution condemning the Israeli invasion of Lebanon.[28] Iraqi prime minister Nuri al-Maliki made a strong statement condemning the invasion.[29] He got a lot of flak about that when he came to the United States. Some Democratic congressional representatives boycotted him because he dared to condemn a U.S.-Israeli invasion of another country.[30] You're not allowed to do that. For a liberal Democrat, that's outrageous.

The relentless carnage and mayhem in Iraq has even driven the Pulitzer Prize–winning columnist of the New York Times *Thomas Friedman, a big supporter of the invasion, to back off from his earlier position.*[31] *Where do you see U.S. policy in Iraq going?*

The United States has a real dilemma. All the talk about withdrawal strategies is essentially worthless unless we face a fundamental point: the United States cannot easily withdraw from Iraq. It cannot leave Iraq as a sovereign, independent state. "Cannot" is too strong, but it would be an immense defeat, nothing like Vietnam. The analogies are worthless. In the case of Vietnam, they could destroy the country, walk out, and basically win the war. Those were their major objectives: killing a "virus" that might "infect" others by independent development, maybe undermining the U.S. position in much of Asia if the "infection" spread. They didn't achieve the maximal objectives in Vietnam, but they achieved the main ones. You can't do that in Iraq. It's much too valuable. Not only in itself—Iraq has the second-largest oil reserves in the world, and very accessible ones—but because of its position right in the center of the world's main energy-producing regions. Iraq borders Iran and Saudi Arabia. It would be a nightmare for them to leave Iraq to its own population, which would, of course, have a Shiite majority and would tighten its relations with Iran, as it's already begun doing.

By a strange accident of geography, the major energy reserves of the world happen to be in Shiite-dominated areas. Saudi Arabia has the world's major energy reserves. Saudi reserves are concentrated mostly right on

the border with Iraq, which has a very large Shiite population that has been bitterly repressed by the U.S.-backed
tyranny and is being spurred to move for greater rights,
maybe even autonomy, by the fact that Iraqi Shiites are
now gaining some degree of control over policy in Iraq.
So you have the possibility of a kind of loose Shiite
alliance—including mostly Shiite Iran, Shiite Iraq, and
the Shiite corner of Saudi Arabia—independent of Washington and controlling most of the world's energy.

As if that isn't bad enough, this alliance could well
turn toward the East. The United States can intimidate Europe, but it can't intimidate China, which is one of the reasons for the fears about China. The Chinese have been
around for three thousand years, and just won't be intimi-
dated. The United States tells the Chinese to back off in the
Middle East, but they continue to invest. When President
Hu Jintao of China visited here last year, the Bush administration thought they could insult him by denying him a
state dinner; they could just have a state lunch.[32] He was
polite. Then he turned the insult around very elegantly by
flying from Washington to Saudi Arabia, where he was
royally welcomed.[33] He made new investment and trade
relations with Saudi Arabia. China is now one of Saudi
Arabia's leading trading partners and is providing them
with military equipment. This must terrify the civilian
planners in the Pentagon. Saudi Arabia is the chief jewel.

All these factors are related to the question of withdrawal from Iraq. It's not a technical question of how you

get the troops out. It has little to do with civil war in Iraq. The United States is really not too concerned about that. In fact, the occupation is probably increasing the civil war. The United States has real motives in staying. And you can't present sensible plans if you don't pay attention to the motives. The main motive is that a sovereign, mildly democratic Iraq would be an utter catastrophe for U.S. planners.

Neoconservative stalwart Bill Kristol recently suggested in the Weekly Standard *that, in response to "Iranian aggression," the United States should seriously consider "a military strike against Iranian nuclear facilities."*[34]

As Kristol certainly knows, the shoe is on the other foot. The Iranian government has been proposing negotiations for years. We now know, and he undoubtedly knows, that in 2003 the moderate Khatami government, with the approval of the hard-line clerical rulers, offered to negotiate all outstanding issues with the United States.[35] That included nuclear issues. It also included a two-state settlement for the Israel-Palestine problem, which, as I mentioned, Iran officially supports. The Bush administration didn't reject the negotiation offer. It didn't even reply to it. Its response was to censure the Swiss diplomat who brought the offer.[36]

It's the United States that's refusing negotiations. The big hoopla that Iran is now willing to negotiate seriously because Condoleezza Rice has shifted policy is not true.[37] Iran's government is not a nice one. There are all kinds of hideous things you can say about it. But the fact is, on the nuclear issue, they are the ones who offered negotiations. They are the ones who said that they would accept the two-state settlement on Israel-Palestine. But the United States is willing to "negotiate" only if Iran concedes the result of the negotiations before the negotiations begin. The negotiations are conditional on Iran stopping uranium enrichment, which it's legally entitled to do, but which is supposed to be the goal of negotiations.[38] So, yes, we'll negotiate if they first concede in advance. And with a gun pointed at their heads, because we won't withdraw the threats against Tehran. Washington has made that very clear. We continue the threats, which are a violation of the UN Charter. In other words, the United States is still refusing to negotiate.

The issue of enriching uranium to weapons grade is a very serious problem. The fate of the species depends on it. If such enrichment continues, we may not survive much longer. There are proposals as to how to deal with the problem. The major one comes from Mohamed ElBaradei, the highly respected head of the International Atomic Energy Agency and Nobel Prize laureate. His proposal is that production of weapons-grade fissile materials be placed under international control and supervision. Anyone who wants to apply for fissile materials can apply to the IAEA for peaceful use.[39] That's a very sensible proposal. As far as I'm aware, there is only one country in the world that has accepted it—Iran. Try to find a reference to that somewhere.

David Korten has a new book out called The Great Turning.[40] *He describes a perfect storm that is looming consisting of three elements: peak oil, climate change, and the collapse of the U.S. dollar.*

Those are all problems, but I think a much more serious one than any of them is the threat of nuclear war. It's not talked about much except in professional circles. If you read the literature by strategic analysts on disarmament, nuclear war is regarded as a serious and growing threat, a threat that's been very sharply increased by the Bush administration's aggressive militarism. And this is not an exotic position. When you get somebody like Robert McNamara warning that current policies are leading to what he called "apocalypse soon," you know this is very serious.[41]

The threat of environmental destruction is also very serious, but it's not as imminent—though the longer we delay in dealing with it, the worse it will be.

As far as the collapse of the dollar is concerned, that's sort of a mixed story. Almost every economist knows that the United States is going to have to do something about the huge trade deficit. And there is only one thing you can do, and that is to weaken the dollar, which will increase inflation and the cost of commodities for consumers, but also could lead to a rise in exports and in manufacturing jobs.

As for peak oil, that might actually be a blessing if it's close. People talk about it as a catastrophe, but what they're failing to notice is that continued use of oil could cause a worse catastrophe, maybe only one generation from now. Oil is finite. So at some point it will no longer be economical to use oil. When that will be, nobody really knows. There are many ambiguities, including whether it's not going to be economically possible to refine oil from tar sands or to exploit other oil that's currently hard to access. It may turn out that Venezuela has the largest reserves in the world, by some measures.[42] It's just very hard to get to. But peak oil will come.

If this situation leads to sensible steps toward reconstructing our society and we accommodate to the fact that we cannot keep polluting the atmosphere, we cannot keep destroying the environment or else we'll all die; if that happens sooner, fine. If it means that the Bush administration or a successor administration will mitigate this impending catastrophe, that would be good. And it may even be good for the economy, contrary to what's almost always said. Conservation, for example, is in many ways good for the economy. These are measures that can be undertaken right away. We can examine alternative energy resources and a change in lifestyle, which is not necessarily harmful. There is nothing great about being able to sit in a traffic jam in New York in your Hummer. It's not the peak of existence.

There are plenty of other real threats. The health care problem is very severe. The United States has the worst health care system in the industrial world and costs about twice per capita that of other industrial societies, with some of the worst outcomes in the industrial world.[43] And costs are continuing to go up for reasons that people understand pretty well: the extraordinary power of the pharmaceutical industries, which are state-subsidized but want to ensure that drug prices keep escalating, and the privatized health system, which is extremely inefficient and costly. That's another serious problem, which our children and grandchildren are left to worry about, unless we deal with it the way the large majority of the population wants: a universal health care program. It's not utopian exactly to say that we should have a system at least as efficient as that of other industrial societies.

There has been a persistence of various theories about September 11 alleging direct or indirect Bush administration participation in the attacks. Why do you think that is?

First of all, I don't think much of those theories, but I am bombarded with letters about this subject. It's not only a huge industry but it's kind of a fanatic industry. Many other people think I ought to change my priorities. But of the couple hundred letters I'm getting every day, the

flood that's really abusive, which says, "It's your respon-
sibility to set this as your highest priority and to drop
everything else," is coming from the "9/11 truth" people.
It's almost a kind of religious fanaticism.

There are some questions you have to ask. One has to
do with the physical evidence. There are the unexplained
coincidences, personal accounts, and so on, which don't
amount to much. That's found in any complex world event.
With regard to the physical evidence, can you become a
highly qualified civil and mechanical engineer and expert
in the structure of buildings by spending a couple of hours
on the Internet? If you can, we can get rid of the civil and
mechanical engineering departments at MIT. Why go to
the university? If you really believe any of this evidence,
then there is an easy way to proceed. Go to specialists who
can evaluate it. You may have found one physicist somewhere, though as far as I know no one has been willing to
submit anything to a serious professional peer-reviewed
journal. But that aside, you can go to the civil and mechanical engineering departments. Maybe the "9/11 truth movement" believes they're all in on the conspiracy. If it's that
vast, we may as well forget it. These people claim that
they're afraid. There is nothing to be afraid of. It's one of
the safest positions to take among those who are critical of
power, as anyone with experience in these matters knows.
In fact, it's treated rather tolerantly by power centers.

Which takes us to another question. Why is this discussion of 9/11 treated so tolerantly? I suspect people in

positions of power like it. It's diverting enormous amounts of energy away from the real crimes of the administration, which are far more serious. Suppose they did blow up the World Trade Center? By their standards, that's a minor crime. Increasing the threat of nuclear war and environmental disaster is a far worse crime, which might lead to extinction of the species. Take the invasions of Iraq and Lebanon. Or look at what they're doing to working people in the United States. We can go on and on. They're committing real crimes, and there is very little protest about it. One of the reasons—not the only one, of course—is that so much potential activist energy is directed into 9/11 discussions. From the point of view of power centers, that's great. We'll give these people exposure on C-SPAN and have their books right up front at the local bookstores. A pretty tolerant reaction. We sort of say we think it's a bad joke, but you don't get the kind of reaction you do when you really go after hard issues.

So, yes, it's a terrible drain of energy away from much more serious problems. And I don't think the evidence is serious. I don't think the people who are presenting the physical evidence are even in a position to evaluate it. These are hard technical questions. What doesn't seem to be understood is that there is a reason scientists do experiments. They don't just take videotapes of what's happening out the window. The reason is that what's happening out the window involves so many variables you don't understand what you're getting in this complex mess. You can find all kinds of unexplained coincidences, apparent violations of the laws of nature. Even with controlled experiments, there are plenty of problems. You read the letters columns of science journals, you will find countless examples. So the fact that you're finding out this happened, that happened, and so on, doesn't mean anything.

The "Who benefits from 9/11?" argument has little force. I think in my first interview after 9/11, I made the not very brilliant prediction that every power system in the world would immediately exploit this for their own purposes.[44] So Russia will step up its atrocities in Chechnya, Israel will in the West Bank, Indonesia will in Aceh, China in western China. In the United States, it was exploited, as we know, but also in ways that weren't very well advertised.

One of the ways 9/11 was exploited was just reported in an excellent investigative report in the *Wall Street Journal* about how major corporations used 9/11 to give their top management huge stock options.[45] The stock market was closed for a couple of days, and everybody feared that when it reopened, it was going to collapse. So they gave out stock options at a very low price timed for the day of the opening. And, of course, the stocks were going to go back up. So it was a huge bonanza for the CEOs and top management. That's one way to exploit 9/11. And there are others. Almost every government instituted measures to control their own population more intensively, and so on. The Bush administration did, too. So the fact that some people benefited doesn't tell you anything.

The whole idea completely lacks credibility. If there were any truth to the claims about 9/11, it would require a huge conspiracy, involving the airline industries, the media, the faking of the planes. A lot of people in the administration would have had to know. You could never get away with it. Even a dictatorship couldn't get away with it. It's a very chancy operation. The chances of a leak are pretty high. It would be exposed in no time. If there was even the slightest leak, these guys would be lined up before firing squads, and that's the end of the Republican Party forever. And all to gain what? A pretext for what they were going to do anyway, and they always could have found another pretext.

So what is the real appeal of these claims about 9/11?

I think it's a lot like the appeal of the fundamentalist evangelical religions. People are very suspicious, rightly. They don't trust institutions. The society has been atomized. There is plenty of activism and popular organization, but the unions are mostly gone, and political parties don't exist. It's one of the reasons why most of the activism comes out of churches.

So, you have people who don't like what's going on, who have been through very hard times, who don't trust anything, don't like what's happening, and have no way to react. So they latch on to something. And the Internet has a dangerous effect. The Internet is terrifically useful for getting information, for activism, for all sorts of things. But it has a downside. One person can come up with theory on a blog, and it has minimal credibility, but then five other people see it, and pretty soon you get exponential growth and have a huge industry reinforcing itself. There are a number of these industries. The 9/11 movement is one of them, but there are plenty of others. It's easy for that to happen in an atomized, depoliticized society.

I get a flood of e-mail. And quite a lot of it, many letters a day, comes from very sincere, honest people saying, "Tell me what I can do." These e-mails are almost always from wealthy, privileged sectors. Not the super-wealthy, but from people who are privileged enough to sit down in the evening and write a letter to someone. In a third world country, people don't say "Tell me what to do," they tell you what they're doing. But in a place where people have a very high level of freedom by comparative standards, people always ask, "What can I do?" And then they say, here's something I can do. I can become a qualified civil engineer in an hour, and prove that Bush blew up the World Trade Center.

I'm pretty sure that in Washington they must be clapping. A couple of years ago, I came across a Pentagon document that was about declassification procedures. Among other things, it proposed that the government should periodically declassify information about the Kennedy assassination.[46] Let people trace whether Kennedy was killed by the mafia, so activists will go off on a wild-goose chase instead of pursuing real problems or getting organized. It wouldn't shock me if thirty years from now we discover in the declassified record that the 9/11 industry was also being fed by the administration.

THREE

LATIN AMERICA: STIRRINGS IN THE SERVANTS' QUARTERS

CAMBRIDGE, MASSACHUSETTS (SEPTEMBER 29, 2006)

In Hegemony or Survival, *you quote Thucydides, "Large nations do what they wish, while small nations accept what they must."*[1]

In my opinion, that's one of the two leading principles of international relations. Most of international relations theory you can more or less dispense with, I think, but that's a principle that is operative in international affairs. And I think it should be paired with a principle brought up by Adam Smith, who is greatly revered but not very much read. He pointed out—he was talking about England, of course—that the "principal architects" of state policy, the "merchants and manufacturers," make sure that their own interests are "most particularly attended to," however "grievous" the consequences for others, including the people of England.[2] That's the second principle of international relations. If you just think of these two simple axioms, you can account for a fair amount of state policy, almost independent of which state it is.

A lot of attention was paid to Hugo Chávez's speech in New York at the United Nations on September 20, 2006. He referred to Bush as "the devil" and made comments about "sulfur" coming from the podium.[3] Here in the United States, there is a tendency to attack Bush personally, with a lot of name-calling. Do you think that's useful?

First of all, I disagree with your first statement. I think no attention was paid to Chávez's speeches, either at the General Assembly on September 20, which was at least mentioned, or the much more important one he gave at the General Assembly last year.[4] In his 2005 speech, Chávez talked about reintroducing the concept of a new international economic order, a proposal that was sponsored by the former colonial countries, the nonaligned movement in the 1970s, and put forward by the United Nations Conference on Trade and Development (UNCTAD), the main UN development agency. This was a very serious program to try to bring the so-called third world into international affairs on a slightly more equal footing. That was shot down very fast. Instead, the rich countries, primarily the United States, instituted almost the opposite, the so-called neoliberal order. Those are important issues for most of the world—but not here.

Chávez also brought up crucial questions about UN reform, suggested that the United Nations be placed in an international city, in the south, where most of the world's population is. He brought up questions about energy consumption. Venezuela is an oil producer, of course, but he said there is far too much oil used for energy production, which is very destructive of the environment. Socioeconomic orders have to be significantly modified, particularly in the rich industrial countries, to reduce the catastrophic consequence of using oil for energy production, cars, heating, and so on. He talked about the UN millennium goals.[5] And he reiterated the importance of maintaining the constraints on the threat and use of force in international affairs in the UN Charter. Here he's re-endorsing the UN High-level Panel on Threats, Challenges, and Change.[6] That was a very serious speech. As far as I could see, it received barely any coverage at all.

As to the recent speech mentioning Bush as the devil and talking about the smell of sulfur, I don't think it's constructive. I don't like Donald Rumsfeld's rhetoric when he compares Chávez to Hitler or Nancy Pelosi's when she calls him a "thug."[7] But that's not very interesting. If there really were newspapers in the country, they would talk about Rumsfeld's policies and Chávez's policies, not what rhetoric they use. That's gossip.

To get back to your question, though, about people here calling Bush names, that's very constructive—for the radical right. It is as if these people have been programmed by Karl Rove. Rove wants to have the liberal critics ridicule Bush because he says "nucular" and "misunderestimate" and talks with a probably fake Texas accent. In fact, my suspicion is he's probably been trained to make grammatical errors—he didn't talk like that at Yale—so he'll be ridiculed by liberals, and then he can say, "See, those elite liberals who run the world and are sitting around drinking French wine and eating quiche don't understand us ordinary guys." Regular guys like the guy working on the assembly line and George Bush, who is going back to his ranch to cut brush. That's all part of the imagery. So if you want to contribute to that imagery and to the success of the ultra-right, then you should make fun of George Bush's accent and engage in other forms of ridicule. But that rhetoric is destructive and childish. And the same holds true of everyone else's rhetoric.

What's important is the content, which was systematically evaded in the discussions of Chávez's recent speech. If I had the resources, I'd like to do a media search and see if there were any references to the substance of his remarks. After all, if you read the *New York Times* news account, what's called a news account, it was mostly kind of gossip and making fun of the speech. However, the *Times* did include a sentence that was interesting. The reporter said Chávez received "loud applause that lasted so long that the organization's officials had to tell the cheering group to cut it out."[8] Any serious journalist or commentator would ask the next question: Why did Chávez receive prolonged applause? Is it because he called George Bush a devil? No. It was because he was expressing a point of view that happens to be very widely accepted in the world. In fact, it's the overwhelmingly dominant position. Chávez's views are called "controversial." It's quite the opposite. It's the views of the U.S. media and commentators that are controversial.

There is nothing controversial about Chávez saying that the United States is one of the greatest threats to peace in the world. Take a look at polls in Europe—when people are asked to list the major threats to peace, the United States is way in the lead, far ahead of Iran or anybody else.[9] So, unless you define the world as the *New York Times* editorial board, and others in the same circles, his statement is not controversial. What's controversial is the U.S. position of saying it's controversial. Those are the kinds of reports that newspapers should have run after Chávez's speech.

Just about every article you see about Venezuela calls Chávez a "tinpot dictator." By what standards is he a dictator? He's been repeatedly elected in elections certified as free and fair. The media in Venezuela bitterly condemn him in terms that are virtually unimaginable in the United States. There was a military coup that briefly overthrew him, supported by the top media and by the Bush administration.[10] They've had a series of referendums, all of which Chávez has won handily, without any coercion that anyone knows about, certainly not by international standards. Nothing like the gentleman from Kazakhstan who is being welcomed at the White House today, Nursultan Nazarbayev, who is really a dictator, and a brutal one.[11] But that's fine. You might hear a few remarks about how maybe he's not perfect or democracy has to come slowly, but he's getting the red-carpet treatment.

The most important question is what do Venezuelans think about Chávez? That's the question you ask about a political leader. And we know the answer. In the years that he's been in office, support for the elected government has steadily risen. It is now the highest in Latin America.[12] That's of some interest. The next question is: Why has support grown for Chávez? It's because there are social programs that are helping the great majority of the population. Venezuela should be a very rich country. It has plenty of resources. It has a very small super-rich elite, some highly privileged sectors, and a huge mass of extremely impoverished people who apparently believe—you can argue about whether they're right or not—that this is the first government that's ever cared about them. Is that undemocratic?

In fact, what's called "undemocratic" by the United States is extremely interesting. For example, when Evo

Morales in Bolivia made moves toward nationalization of Bolivia's resources, he was condemned as authoritarian, dictatorial, attacking democracy.[13] But did it matter that he was supported by about 95 percent of the population?[14] Is that what "dictatorial" means? We have a particular concept of democratic, which means "do what we say." Then a country is democratic, or is becoming democratic. But if a country does what the population wants, it's not democratic. It's shocking that people can't see this.

Thomas Friedman writes that Chávez "uses Venezuela's oil riches to try to sway democratic elections in Latin America and promote an economic populism that will eventually lead his country into a ditch."[15]

It's undoubtedly true that Chávez is trying to influence elections. Is that something new? You think that we don't try to influence elections? Not only does the U.S. government work desperately to influence elections in other countries, but if they come out the wrong way, we punish the population. Is Chávez doing that?

If you don't think countries should influence other countries' elections, then shut down the National Endowment for Democracy and shut down the State Department, which is right now, for example, intervening massively in the Nicaraguan election. The ambassador—on Condoleezza Rice's orders, I presume—is telling the people of Nicaragua, in effect, "If you don't vote the way we say, we're going to strangle you."[16]

As to whether his policies will lead Venezuela into a ditch, Thomas Friedman is hardly an authority. The economic policies he supports have been a disaster for most of the global south. If you take a look at the last twenty-five years, growth rates have sharply declined in countries that have adopted the policies he loves. The countries that have done very well—China, South Korea, Taiwan—have done so by violating the rules that Friedman advocates. These countries radically violated International Monetary Fund and World Bank rules—the Washington consensus, which he praises—and they grew. On the other hand, the countries that observed neoliberal rules rigorously had an extremely sharp decline in economic growth and just about every other macroeconomic measure.

In fact, the United States doesn't follow the rules that it imposes on others. During the last twenty-five years, to the extent that there has been a limited imposition of neoliberalism in the United States, it's been the worst prolonged period in U.S. economic history. In a period of twenty-five years with no wars and no major recessions, real wages have stagnated for the majority of the population.[17] When did that last happen? It's true that the economy has been great for Thomas Friedman and his friends—and for people like me, people in our income bracket. For the top half of one percent of the population, it's just magnificent. You can call it a golden age, if you like. But that's certainly not true for most of the population.

Take Friedman's favorite example, India, which just dazzles him. He goes on and on about the marvelous labs in Hyderabad. It's true. I've been in the labs in Hyderabad. They're as good as MIT's. But a couple of miles away, the rate of peasant suicides has risen very sharply as a result of the same policies.[18] You turn government funding into support for software engineering and take it away from rural development—support for farmers, irrigation, rural credit. So, you drive farmers to export production. Instead of producing food for the country and themselves, they produce, say, cotton, which requires high inputs, fertilizer and plenty of water, which are not available. And the prices fluctuate radically. So one year you may make a lot of money and the next year you may make nothing. In agribusiness, it doesn't matter that much. It kind of levels out and you have other crops. But if you're a poor farmer and you can't sell your crops one year, you can't tell your children, "Don't worry, we don't have to eat this year. Maybe we'll eat next year." So you go into debt. Since the government doesn't provide rural credit, thanks to the policies Friedman lauds, you borrow from a usurer at 40 percent interest. Then the next year you can't pay him, so you've got to sell off your land. Pretty soon your children are starving and you can do nothing. That's why the rate of peasant suicides is sharply rising within eyesight of the marvels that Friedman describes.

As the journalist P. Sainath has pointed out, for the first time in Indian history there is mass migration from the countryside.[19] There always was migration during harvests. This is different. People are fleeing the devastated countryside, where the large majority lives, and essentially pouring into the Mumbai slums. The most serious economic analyses—not the rave reviews on the op-ed page of the *Times* but real analyses—indicate that maybe 80 percent of the population or so is in the informal economy, which is not even counted.[20] In states such as Uttar Pradesh, which has about the same population as Pakistan, the conditions for women are probably worse than under the Taliban. Go around India, and that's what you find. There is growth, which is good. They're improving roads, they have a big software program, they do have great labs. But for most of the population, it's hardly heaven. Very far from it. And India is one of the better stories, because it didn't observe the neoliberal rules. The Indian government has maintained control over capital flows and finance, and has violated IMF rules in numerous ways.

The countries in Latin America and southern Africa that adhered to the rules, on the other hand, are the worst disasters. These figures are muddled in the pronouncements by the World Bank and by many economists who argue that growth has really improved greatly and poverty has been reduced by neoliberal rules. The way they get these results is by mixing together two quite different things: one is export orientation and the other is following the Washington consensus, the neoliberal rules. So China, which has a population of one billion people, has been dedicated to export promotion but has also violated the neoliberal rules. If you muddle all of this together, you can say, "Well, the neoliberal rules work because a billion Chinese had a high growth rate," forgetting that they had a high growth rate by violating the neoliberal rules. This kind of deception is going on all the time.

The rigorous application of neoliberal rules typically requires dictatorship, because people don't like them. The most rigorous application was in Chile after the Pinochet coup in 1973. That's when economists from the University of Chicago became involved. They could do anything they wanted. The country was under the rule of a vicious police state, so nobody could object. By 1982, under the influence of the "Chicago Boys," Chile suffered probably the worst economic collapse of its history. The government had to step in and bail out virtually the whole of private industry and the banks. In fact, Chileans called this "the Chicago road to socialism."[21] The state ended up owning more of the economy under Pinochet than it had under Salvador Allende. That was the great neoliberal experiment. Finally, the military itself couldn't handle the situation anymore and turned it back over to civilians. And Chile slowly recovered, with a mixed economy of a complex sort. It's called a "free-market miracle," but in fact the economy relies very heavily on a nationalized copper company, Codelco (Corporación Nacional del Cobre de Chile), which was originally nationalized by Allende. Pinochet didn't dare privatize it. Codelco is very efficient, apparently, and is the biggest copper producer in the world.[22] It also provides far more revenues to the state than the private companies, subsidizing social programs and other expenses. So if copper prices go up, Chile does fine. And in other ways, the economy is somewhat liberated from the orthodox prescriptions that had devastated it.

The same is true in neighboring Argentina, which rigorously followed IMF rules—that means Treasury Department rules, the ones that Thomas Friedman extols—and created a total catastrophe. Finally, Nestor Kirchner was elected. He radically violated IMF rules, and there was a very significant recovery. Argentineans are now ridding themselves of the IMF, thanks in part to the fact that Venezuela helped them buy out their debt.[23]

That's the real world. It's different if you're eating in elegant restaurants, meeting your rich friends, and reading the editorials in the *Wall Street Journal*.

In Hegemony or Survival, *you say that there is a "severe democracy deficit" in the United States.*[24]

I've discussed this in more detail in a later book, *Failed States*, running extensively through public opinion studies and actual policy.[25] There is an enormous gap between public opinion and policy. In 2005, for example, right after the federal budget was announced, the Program on International Policy Attitudes, which also studies domestic issues, did an extensive poll on what people thought the budget ought to be. It turned out to be the inverse of the actual budget: where federal funding was going up, an overwhelming majority wanted it to go down. The public opposed increases in military spending overall and supplemental spending for Iraq and Afghanistan, which is going up even more now. Where the budget was going down—social expenditures, health, renewable energy, veterans' benefits, the United Nations—right across the board, the public wanted spending to increase.[26]

I asked a friend to see how many newspapers in the country reported this. Apparently not one. This is extremely important news. The population is radically opposed to government policy. Isn't that important news in a democracy? What does that tell us about American democracy?

Just a few weeks ago, Paul Waldman had an op-ed in the leading liberal newspaper in the country, the *Boston Globe*, telling Democrats that they just don't get it.[27] He said Democrats still believe issues are important in elections—which happens to be false, since they don't really think that—but the Republicans understand that issues don't matter. It's imagery that matters. So what the Democrats have to do, Waldman says, is completely toss out whatever relics of democracy they have and advertise their candidates like lifestyle drugs on television. Then we'll have real democracy. The popular view these days is that we have to understand how to "frame" issues better. All we have to do is change our rhetoric and to be as deceitful as the Republicans are. Let's forget about issues, and just use the proper rhetoric.

When I was driving home the other day and listening to NPR—my masochist streak—they happened to have a long segment on Barack Obama.[28] It was very favorable, really enthusiastic. Here is a new star rising in the political firmament. I was listening to see if the report would say anything about his position on issues—any issue. Nothing. It was just about his image. I think they may have had a couple words about him being in favor of doing something about the climate. What are his positions? It just doesn't matter. You read the articles. It's the same. He gives hope. He looks right into your eyes when you talk to him. That's what's considered significant. Not "Should we control our own resources? Should we nationalize our resources? Should we have water for people? Should we have health care systems? Should we stop carrying out aggression?" No. That's not mentioned. Because our electoral system, our political system, has been driven to such a low level that issues are completely marginalized. You're not supposed to know the information about candidates.

A number of people are concerned about election fraud, citing Florida in 2000 and Ohio in 2004.

First of all, personally I think those concerns are misplaced. Yes, there is electoral fraud. It's always been true. John F. Kennedy, for example, was apparently elected on the basis of voter fraud in Chicago, which shifted Illinois to him. But the much more serious problem is that elections aren't really taking place at all. When you have two candidates whose party managers disguise their positions, if they even have positions, so that the population doesn't know what the issues are and instead is being deluded by imagery, you end up getting what we usually do, something like a statistical tie. It's kind of like coin flipping. If it turns out that the coin is a little bit biased, that's not the problem. The real problem is that there was no election in any serious sense.

In 2000, it seems obvious that there was vote tampering. In 2004, it's possible that vote tampering helped put into office an extremely radical reactionary statist clique that is doing immense harm to the world. In that sense voter fraud is important. But if you're thinking about the functioning of democracy, what's more important is that we don't have real elections.

Take, say, the congressional elections in November. Every seat in the House of Representatives is coming up for a vote. But how many seats are being seriously contested in the next election? Maybe 5 or 10 percent.[29]

Incumbents almost always win, because they have the most funding. In fact, you can pretty well predict the outcome of elections with quite high probability just by looking at the relative amount of funding available to the candidates, which primarily means how much business support are they getting. Is that a democratic election, where a handful of seats are even contested? Even James Madison, who was not a democrat, would be turning over in his grave.

Let's go back to Latin America. You've reviewed some of the history between the United States and Venezuela. Talk about Juan Vicente Gómez and Marcos Pérez Jiménez.

Maybe I should add to the maxims of Thucydides and Adam Smith a third rule of international affairs. That is, the people who hold the clubs insist on historical amnesia. For us, history is kind of old, antiquated, boring stuff. Who cares about that? Let's march on to a glorious future. But the people who are hit by the clubs tend to remember history, because they know that it matters and they see it being reenacted. Venezuela is a case in point. Venezuela was pretty much a British protectorate. When the oil age began, at around the end of the First World War, Woodrow Wilson, in another act of idealism, kicked the British out of Venezuela, took it over, supported the vicious Gómez dictatorship, and put Venezuelan oil under U.S. control. So everything was fine. That continued right through Pérez Jiménez. He got a medal from the Eisenhower administration. Again, a brutal dictator, but Venezuelan oil was kept available, controlled pretty much by U.S. corporations. And not just oil. Venezuela has other natural resources, and the small Venezuelan elite was enriching itself by collaborating with the United States. They pretty much ran the government. There was a little deviation, with support for Rómulo Betancourt and a couple of other social democrats, but that's pretty much the story.

Under the last pre-Chávez government, Venezuela was a neoliberal disaster. Poverty was imposed at such a level that there were massive riots. Chávez himself took part in an attempted military coup and spent some time in jail.[30] The growth rate collapsed. The country was in a disaster. That's all part of Venezuelans' memory. Just as the 2002 coup is part of their memory, just as the current measures of subversion against the Chávez government are part of their memory.

Let's just imagine that Iran had supported a military coup in the United States that overthrew the government before it was restored by popular reaction. Suppose that Iran came into the United States to "support democracy" by pouring money into what they would call pro-democracy organizations, namely, those opposed to the government. How would we like it? Would we call this "democracy promotion"?

Incidentally, it's not just Venezuela where historical amnesia is crucial. It's every other place, too. Take Iran.

For our history, there is one event, the hostage taking in 1979, but Iranians don't see it the same way. Iranian history includes over half a century of unremitting torment of the people of Iran by the United States, beginning with the overthrow of the parliamentary government in 1953 in a CIA and British coup, which reinstated the vicious tyrant Shah Reza Pahlavi, whom London and Washington supported all through his atrocities. There was virtually not a word about the shah's torture, the Savak atrocities, and so on in the U.S. media.[31] Nothing until 1979.

Finally, Jimmy Carter went to Tehran in 1977 and praised "the great leadership of the shah" and the "admiration and love" the people have for him.[32] Carter's comments infuriated a lot of Iranians. As soon as the shah was overthrown in 1979, the Carter administration almost immediately tried to instigate a military coup. When that didn't work, the Reagan administration turned to Saddam Hussein, who invaded Iran. The Reagan administration took Iraq off the list of states sponsoring terrorism so that they could provide their friend Saddam with substantial aid—including means to develop weapons of mass destruction, such as chemical weapons—and ended up with hundreds of thousands of Iranians being slaughtered, all with the support of the United States. This went on right through Saddam Hussein's worst atrocities. Finally, Washington virtually entered the war directly and Iran capitulated, figuring that it couldn't fight the United States.[33] That's all part of their memory in Iran.

Also part of their memory, I presume, is that the support for Saddam Hussein continued. In fact, in 1989, after the war with Iran had ended, the United States invited Iraqi nuclear engineers to come here for advanced training in how to develop nuclear weapons.[34] I doubt if Iranians have forgotten that. It might make them a little cynical when they see the alleged concern about Iranian nuclear weapons. That's over half a century of torture. Does that matter? It matters to people in Iran. It doesn't matter to the guys who hold the clubs.

Venezuela, along with Argentina, Cuba, and Uruguay, have started Telesur, which is a Latin American television channel that seeks to present news more from a grassroots perspective. It's been described as kind of an Al Jazeera in Spanish. And the other initiative that Chávez has undertaken—which, again, is called "controversial" in the United States—is supplying home heating oil at discount prices to low-income communities in Boston, not very far from where we're sitting, the South Bronx, and other poor areas.

Let's start with the heating oil. A group of U.S. politicians approached the major oil companies and asked politely if they could provide cheaper oil to help poor families last winter because prices were really high and people couldn't afford heating. Only one responded—Citgo, a

Venezuelan-run company. Citgo agreed to provide oil at cheap rates to poor people around the United States.[35] That was bitterly condemned by the government, by the media, as Chávez just using his oil wealth to gain support—as if our foreign aid is totally altruistic. We never give aid for any political or other purpose. Chávez is also providing cheap oil to the Caribbean and South America. The Caribbean countries receive oil through the PetroCaribe program at basically discount prices, with cheap credit.[36] Yes, that's buying influence, undoubtedly.

You could say the same about Operation Miracle in the Caribbean, a project in which, with Venezuelan financial support, Cuban doctors are going to places like Jamaica to provide health care.[37] Right now they're concentrating on blindness, finding people who could have their sight restored by advanced surgical treatments. They're taking them to Cuba to treat them. The patients come back to Jamaica, and they can see. Cuba and Venezuela are doing exactly what we were all taught we're supposed to do in graduate courses in economics: they're pursuing their comparative advantage. The comparative advantage of Venezuela is oil. The comparative advantage of Cuba is highly trained, skilled professionals: doctors, teachers, nurses. So they're basically exchanging them in Venezuela and Cuba, but also elsewhere.

You think that has an effect on Jamaicans? You bet it does. This is just another example of Venezuelan imperialism, as if we couldn't do the same thing. But if we were to do it, it would be called magnificent humanitarianism. When Cuba and Venezuela do it, then it's two tinpot dictators trying to run the world and destroy us. But it matters to the people who receive the aid, just as buying up a large part of the Argentine debt to rid them of the IMF means something to people in Argentina. The pipeline that Venezuela has proposed running down to Argentina, if it is implemented, would be of great benefit to the countries of Latin America, a method of unification, of moving toward some sort of energy integration and independence.[38] The United States hates the idea, of course.

About Telesur, there is a very important background there, which of course we have suppressed here. I mentioned earlier that Chávez had talked at the United Nations about reviving the new international economic order sponsored by the major nonaligned countries— most of the world—and by UNCTAD in the 1970s. There was also another idea, a new international information order. It was sponsored by the United Nations Educational, Scientific, and Cultural Organization (UNESCO) in this case. The idea was to try to give third world countries some sort of input into the international media system, instead of having it totally monopolized by a few rich Western powers, the United States primarily. This was bitterly attacked in the United States. Across the spectrum, it was derided as an effort to end the free press and to control journalists. The attacks were full of the most outrageous lies. The press, like the *New York Times*, would not permit responses by UNESCO officials.[39] Finally, the United States defunded UNESCO to try to prevent third world input into the international information system. They understand. The "free press" means we have a monopoly and you have to shut up and listen to what we say.

So Telesur is attempting to revive aspects of the new international information order. The same is true of Al Jazeera. The U.S.-backed tyrants who run the oil states of the Middle East—Saudi Arabia and the rest of them— hate Al Jazeera. They despise it. And the United States despises Al Jazeera for the same reason: it's an independent voice. You can't have that. The United States bombed Al Jazeera facilities in Kabul and Baghdad and claimed these were accidents.[40] I don't think anybody with their eyes open believes that. When the United States was finally compelled by popular resistance to allow an election in Iraq—they tried to prevent it in every possible way and, of course, are now taking credit for it— but when they couldn't prevent it anymore, they tried to subvert it. The administration has sought in every way to stop Al Jazeera. One of the ways to gain control was by driving them out of Baghdad.[41] You can't have a free election if we don't control everything.

One of the most comical press conferences was when the emir of Qatar came to Washington. He was called on the carpet by Colin Powell, who tried to get him to shut down Al Jazeera. He had a press conference in which, tongue in cheek, he informed the media that in Qatar they believe in this thing called freedom of the press and, of course, it sometimes means that people say things we don't like.[42] The emir of Qatar finally, under U.S. pressure, proposed to privatize the station. The Bush administration said that won't work—you've got to close it down. There cannot be either a public or a private station that is independent of our control. That's our concept of democracy promotion.

Al Jazeera is very widely watched in the Arab world. During the U.S.-Israeli invasion of Lebanon in the summer of 2006, which practically destroyed the country, Al Jazeera's correspondents were right on the ground. They showed the pictures. People saw what was happening. And it has an effect. Now they're trying to open up an English television alternative.[43] The last I heard, they have barely been able to get an entry. I think maybe one cable station somewhere is willing to pick it up. There is going to be tremendous resistance to Al Jazeera having access to the airwaves in English.

Telesur is an issue, too. The United States doesn't have the power to shut it down. And Chávez isn't going to listen to Bush and Rice when they tell him to close Telesur. I don't know what will happen. But it is an alternative. It's a voice that expresses the position of the vast majority of the world's population, at least to some extent, whereas we insist on an information system that is under the control of the rich and powerful and works for their interests.

Could you talk about the significance of Venezuela joining the Mercosur trade area and the general integration that's happening in Latin America? In an article in the International Socialist Review *you wrote, "Venezuela has forged probably the closest relations with China of any Latin American country."*[44] *Why is that important?*

That is very significant. This is the first time since the Spanish conquest that Latin America has begun moves toward independence and integration. I have to qualify that—they have tried it before but were crushed. So, for example, Brazil had a moderately populist democratic government in the early 1960s. The Kennedy administration organized a military coup that imposed a neo-Nazi national security state that was the first of the plague that then spread throughout the continent to Chile, Argentina, Central America, and turned into one huge massacre. So people in Latin America have tried in the past, as they tried to free themselves from Spain. There were many efforts. But this is the first one that has the chance of succeeding, because by now they have extricated themselves to an extent from Western—first European, then U.S.—control. Venezuela is playing a big role in this process, but it's not the only country. We have seen a wave of democratic elections from Venezuela to Argentina with popular participation and a sort of leftist orientation.

As most of South America drifts toward independence and integration, the major means of U.S. control have lost their power. Historically, one method of control was violence, the mailed fist, and another was economic pressure, which in the recent period has been exercised through the IMF, the Treasury Department, and the World Bank. Both are losing their efficacy. The last effort of the United States to support violence, the traditional means, was in Venezuela during the coup in 2002. Washington had to back down and now pretends it didn't have anything to do with the coup. It backed down because of the popular reaction in Venezuela, but also because of the very strong negative reaction in Latin America. In Latin America, people just take democracy more seriously than in the West, certainly the United States.

I wouldn't say the threat of violence is gone. The United States probably has more military forces in Latin America now than at the height of the Cold War. Training of Latin American officers has shot up, the School of the Americas–style training. In fact, I think for the first time, U.S. military spending—what's called aid to Latin America—is higher than the total amount of economic aid from key federal agencies.[45] That never happened in the Cold War. And bases are going up all over the place. Preparations are being made for military action of one sort or another. But Washington doesn't have the capacity that it had in the past. You can't just instigate military dictatorships and then support them. So that's lessened.

The economic strangulation has also lessened. Argentina kicking out the IMF is one example. Meanwhile, integration is going on, slowly. When Venezuela joined Mercosur, President Kirchner of Argentina and Lula da Silva of Brazil hailed it as a great step forward.[46] How meaningful it will be, we have to wait to see. There are a lot of internal problems, but it's the beginnings of integration.

If you look at the history of Latin American countries, they have been very disintegrated. The elites were oriented toward the West. The châteaus were in the Riviera. That's where you take your vacations. Your children went to U.S. and European universities. Even the transportation systems were oriented toward the West. Capital flow went to the West, not into internal investment. But the integration among the countries was very slight. In fact, there was a lot of conflict among Latin American countries. This is beginning to be overcome.

Is there greater south-south integration internationally?

Look at China. It terrifies Washington planners. Why? Because Beijing is going to attack us? No. China is not a military threat. It's building up in response to Bush militarism, but a very slight one. In fact, it has practically no deterrent force. No, China is a threat because it is moving into Latin America, Saudi Arabia, Iran, and other countries, which is driving Washington crazy. They are becoming a major trading partner in Latin America, not just for Venezuela. The raw materials exporters, including Chile and Brazil, are increasing their trade with China, which in turn invests in their economies. Meanwhile, Venezuela is trying to diversify its oil exports so they're not so dependent on sales to a very hostile United States. It's natural and sensible. A lot of the exports are being diversified to Latin America, but also to China.[47] And the U.S. government is, naturally, very unhappy about that. We're supposed to control resources and markets. Nobody else is.

In some of your talks, usually toward the end, you use the metaphor of looking in the mirror.

We should ask who we are and what we do. For example, when Chávez gets prolonged applause at the General Assembly, instead of ridiculing the rhetoric, we ought to be asking why. What is leading to the fact that in public opinion polls, even in Europe, let alone the rest of the world, people regard the United States as a major threat to world peace and even to their own existence? What is that coming from? It's not enough to say, "They hate us because of our freedom." They don't. So take a look at yourself. See what you're doing. What have we done to Iran for the last fifty years? And what are we doing to Iraq right now?

And why is it that in the polls that appeared just a few days ago, which are so far scarcely reported, it turns out that 70 percent of Iraqis want U.S. troops out within a year and most of the rest want them out not long after. And in Baghdad about two-thirds want them out immediately.[48] Why is that? Look at the studies. They will tell you. It's because there is an overwhelming majority that thinks the United States is contributing to the violence and sectarianism, and the overwhelming majority thinks we're building permanent military bases, which they don't want.[49] Are we? Take a look at the expenditures that are reported. Yes, they're building what they call "semi-permanent" bases, which means permanent as long as we want them there. And they're being built in a manner that entails permanence—deep underground bunkers, and so on.

In fact, the United States isn't even providing the Iraqi army with the means of support for an army, apparently on the assumption that U.S. forces are going to be there to provide the logistics, the support, the backup, the bases, and move in when they have to. The Iraqis don't want that, not only because they think, probably rightly, that we're helping instigate the violence, but because they don't like to be occupied by a foreign power. Would we want to have Iranian bases being built here? So let's look at ourselves in the mirror and ask ourselves why people in the world have this impression of U.S. government policies.

Strikingly, much of the U.S. population has the same impressions as people abroad, but this is excluded effectively from the political system and even the media, which don't report people's attitudes. So let's look at ourselves, see what kind of a country we have. Is that what we want to be? Do we want to be a country that's seen this way and then suffer the consequences? Because we will.

Take, say, the Lebanon war. In Lebanon, about 90 percent of the population regards it as a U.S.-Israeli war, which, of course, it was.[50] We devastated a large part of Lebanon—a large part of it has been made unlivable, saturated with cluster bombs.[51] The effects of bombing fuel storage tanks, creating an oil spill, are apparently causing enormous long-term environmental damage. The environmental minister says that soon most Lebanese will be drinking poisoned water because of the effects of the U.S.-Israeli bombing.[52]

There is an article in Science *magazine on the environmental impact of the attack on Lebanon.*[53]

It gave some technical observations. They analyzed the parts of the oil spill that reached the shore and found very high concentrations of toxic hydrocarbons and other carcinogens and poisons, which they assume must be true everywhere. They also reported that the oil is sinking to the sea bottom, which means it's going to be destroying the food chain. All of this escalates in ways that are familiar. And that's quite apart from the poison clouds over the country from the same oil spills. With that, the cluster bombs, and the vast shelling, a lot of the country was destroyed, and it may remain so for a long time to come. The bombing also destroyed cultural centers, the book-shops. There is an area in Beirut called the cultural zone where the book publishers are mostly located. Lebanon was a cultural center for the Arab world. And the area was flattened. The bookshops are gone.

It is much worse in Iraq. Places with concentrations of bookstores, literary cafés, centers of lively debate that managed to live on during the Saddam Hussein dictator-ship are now empty, wiped out, along with a cultural her-itage that goes back millennia. Here it's just, "Stuff happens."[54] Not there. They care about their culture and civilization and their life.

What's the effect of this going to be? The effect in Lebanon is going to be the same as in Iraq: it will create new generations of jihadis, of people bent on revenge and hatred of the country that caused the destruction. We'll hear from them again. And then we'll wonder, why do they hate us? In fact, if we want to know why, we can go back fifty years. Another reason not to have historical am-nesia. George W. Bush was not the first president to ask why do they hate us. Eisenhower asked it, too. Let's go back and look. Why did they hate us then? The same rea-son they do now. Except more so, because it's gotten worse.

If you look at yourself in the mirror, then maybe you can learn something about yourself. That should be prior-ity number one. Then maybe you can talk about other people. But yes, we should try to understand ourselves, and not just shout jingoistic slogans. Because our dear leader announces that Chávez is a brutal dictator, we have to scream that he's a brutal dictator. Maybe so. But draw your own conclusions, not just because the dear leader pronounced it. We don't have to be voluntary North Koreans.

FOUR

THE UNITED STATES VERSUS THE GOSPELS

CAMBRIDGE, MASSACHUSETTS (DECEMBER 12, 2006)

The New York Times *had a front-page story yesterday about General Augusto Pinochet, the ruler of Chile, who died the previous day.[1] If one were to land in the United States from Mars or some other far-off planet, what kind of information might one get from the nation's premier newspaper about events in Chile?*

If the person from outer space knew the facts, he would assume he had landed in Stalinist Russia, in a totalitarian state. The article makes only passing reference to the U.S. role in the 1973 coup in Chile that brought Pinochet to power. Actually, the United States had been undermining elections in Chile for years, in 1958 and 1964. By 1970, Washington was committed to overthrowing the Allende government. There was a hard track, which would lead to a military coup; and there was a soft track, which was to "make the economy scream," as Nixon told CIA director Richard Helms.[2] The United States engaged directly and extensively with the Chilean upper classes in ensuring that the economy suffered. Chile is just one of a series of coups that the United States either instigated, supported, or directly participated in through the 1960s and 1970s, in the lead-up to the U.S. terrorist war in Central America in the 1980s. There was a plague of repression throughout the continent.

The particular case of Chile happens to be slightly poignant for me personally. I just came back from there a couple of weeks ago. The most accurate statement I have seen about Chile today was by Ariel Dorfman. He called it a "country still full of fear."[3] That's correct. The people experienced seventeen years of dictatorship, and you can feel the fear that remains. Villa Grimaldi was one of the worst of Pinochet's torture chambers. During my recent trip, a man who is now a well-known international lawyer, a professor and human rights activist who was tortured there, took me through it. He took a group of us and went through the process step by step: here's what they did, this is how they tortured us. He said it was years before he could talk about his experience. The torture was hideous. We also met one man who was the lone survivor of the death chamber. After you've been through all of the torture, if they decide they don't want you anymore, they put you in a horrifying death chamber. This one person somehow survived. The tortures were horrifying. He described them in detail.

The torture was all supervised by doctors. Their role was to ensure that the person who was being tortured didn't die, because they had to be kept alive for the next stage of torture. So they would tell the torturers when to stop, administer something to bring the person back to life, and continue the torture. I asked the lawer at one point, "Where are those doctors?" He said, "They're practicing in Santiago." And nobody can think of doing anything about this. It's like having Josef Mengele walking around the streets. That's one aspect of what you see, the fear.

The Chilean writer Juan Hernández Pico wrote about "the culture of terror" that remains and "domesticat[es] . . . the expectations of the majority vis-à-vis alternatives different to those of the powerful."[4] People don't even hope anymore. Friends in Chile talked to me about this. It was once a very lively, exciting country. Now people are isolated. They don't trust each other, they don't want to take any action. The doctors are a particularly grisly case, but there are other examples.

One of the points the *Times* article makes is that even though Pinochet was not a very nice guy, he left this fantastic booming economy guided by the Chicago Boys. The fact of the matter, which the *Times* knows—and if you read carefully, you will notice a phrase referring to it—is that the Chicago Boys not only ran the economy under terror, they drove the country into probably the worst depression in its history. In 1982, the state had to intervene to bail out the private economy. The whole Pinochet period was a total disaster.

Could you talk about the use of the passive voice in reporting on crimes of states?

That's a standard device, to write in the passive. So you have, "People were killed," not "We killed them." Or "They died," not "We murdered them, we tortured them." In fact, there is more that you can say about the Chilean coup. The coup took place on September 11, 1973, which is often called the first 9/11 in South America. If you want to really think of what it was like, let's take a look at our 9/11 and imagine if it was on the same scale as the one in Chile in 1973, the one we were instrumental in perpetrating. To make a sensible analogy, you have to use per capita equivalent numbers because the United States is a much bigger country. So let's imagine that on September 11, 2001, Al Qaeda had bombed the White House, killed the president, instituted a military coup, killed 50,000 to 100,000 people, tortured 700,000, established a terror center in Washington that instigated or supported comparable military coups elsewhere in the hemisphere, murdered and assassinated people they didn't like all over the world. Suppose they brought in a bunch of economists—let's call them the Kandahar Boys—who wrecked the economy, were greatly revered, and then went home to collect their Nobel Prizes. Let's suppose that had happened. Would it have changed the world? Everyone says our September 11 changed the world. But this isn't hypothetical. That's what happend on September 11, 1973.

What's the significance of the fact that Michelle Bachelet, a political prisoner who was exiled and whose father was killed by Pinochet, is now the president of the country?

That's very important. For one thing, culturally and socially Chile is a very conservative country. You're not supposed to have women presidents, especially divorced women presidents. So yes, it is important. Exactly what she'll be able to do is hard to say. The hand of the dictatorship is still very heavy. Just to take another example, Codelco, the state-owned copper company, is required by law to give 10 percent of its income to the army.[5] The great majority doesn't want that anymore, but somehow people don't think they can change it, even though they have the legislature in their hands.

Chile is a very unequal society. I think the inequality is about at the level of Brazil, which is outlandish. When you walk around Santiago, you feel that you're in upscale parts of New York. On the other hand, elsewhere there is tremendous poverty. I met with Indians from the Mapuche area in the south, Aymara in the north, and Quechua in Peru. They have plenty of serious problems. The government to some extent recognizes them, but they're not addressed. And then there are the urban poor and the rural poor. The country's economy is good by international standards, but it's fragile. It's based mostly on primary product export. As long as commodity prices shoot up, it's in pretty good shape.

One of the places I went to is Iquique, in the Andean mining areas. The mining areas are a desert of the kind you can't imagine. There is nothing green, no water, just a flat, kind of brownish sand area with a constant howling wind. The mines now are all closed, but you can imagine how the miners lived. Then they showed me a small concert hall where Luciano Pavarotti and people like that played for the mine owners.

Through the early years of the twentieth century, there were a series of strikes and massacres. At one point, in 1907, miners and their families struck for pennies a day, almost nothing. They marched down to Iquique, a seaside town maybe thirty miles away, and were welcomed by the mine owners and taken into a school and housed. Then they were permitted to have a public meeting in a school yard. The authorities brought in troops and machine-gunned them. Censorship was so heavy that the death toll is unknown. One estimate is that at least one thousand defenseless men, women, and children were murdered. I think that's the worst massacre in labor history. Chilean scholarship describes the massacre as the brutal culmination of a "preventive war" to establish the authority of the state and the owners, to maintain social control, and prevent development of a powerful labor movement. Perhaps it can be properly regarded as a precursor to the hideous era inaugurated on September 11, 1973, with the U.S.-backed Pinochet coup.[6]

That's one of a number of massacres. Technically, it was Chilean, but the British were behind it. In fact, that whole region belongs to Chile mainly because the British backed them in a war with Bolivia and Peru. The British wanted the nitrate mines, which were used for fertilizer and gunpowder. Later, the United States took them over.

Finally locals are beginning to commemorate the Iquique massacre. The younger people in Chile particularly are beginning to come to terms with this history. But we should know about it, too. This is part of Western civilization.

Nicaragua recently had an election in which the former Sandinista leader Daniel Ortega has become president. What's your take on Ortega?

Envío is a magazine published at the Jesuit University in Managua. It's perhaps the best magazine on Central America. Their last issue was on the elections in Nicaragua, and it pointed out that in the preceding elections, in 1996 and 2001, when Ortega seemed to have a chance, there was capital flight and a number of threats. This time, his election was taken very calmly.[7]

To tell you the truth, I never thought much of Ortega in the first place. He completely discredited himself in the 1990s with the pact he made with Arnoldo Alemán, the former Nicaraguan president, who is an ultra-corrupt gangster. The two of them together, with Ortega's control over the Sandinista National Liberation Front, the Sandinista party, and Alemán's party, the Liberal Constitutional Party, could protect Alemán from real punishment and also prevent any real constructive moves being made—not that they were very likely—in the legislature of the government. Ortega appears to have become just another right-wing opportunist. He always was an opportunist. He still has a loyal following among people who have a commitment to the old Sandinista hopes, but it's an illusion.

Nicaragua is a sad place. It's now the second-poorest country in the hemisphere.[8] A very large part of the workforce is abroad, mostly in Costa Rica, sometimes in the United States and elsewhere. There is no development going on, but there is a lot of wealth. If you drive around Managua, you see it's very glitzy. You can buy anything you want. But then you see kids scratching at the windshields asking for a córdoba to get through the night. The country has declined enormously since the United States took it over again in 1990. And Ortega is going with the flow. He and his friends enriched themselves, and they'll pal around with Alemán and the rest of them. I don't think U.S. investors have anything to worry about. They certainly don't seem to be worried. Nor do the corporate elite in Nicaragua, which is super-rich, as in most of the third world.

Nicaragua is the Central American country that most religiously followed IMF rules. So they privatized energy. The other countries didn't. And Nicaragua, predictably, has a terrible energy shortage, much worse than the others.[9] Guatemala is bad enough, but Nicaragua is worse. Costa Rica, the one functioning country in Central America—and incidentally the only one in the region the United States never invaded—has by now moved close to 100 percent sustainable energy.[10]

The foreign-owned company that runs the energy system in Nicaragua has plenty of reserve power, but is not distributing it because it's just not profitable enough. That's the way it works. If you privatize water, you can construct economic models that show you that it's very efficient. But there's a footnote that isn't mentioned. Namely, when you get the prices right, a lot of the population can't pay them, so they don't have water. Nothing's perfect.

There have been major struggles over the issue of water privatization in Bolivia, particularly in Cochabamba, where there was a big uprising that forced out Bechtel and the consortium that was privatizing the water."[11] That was a good example of real globalization. Part of the reason the people of Cochabamba could succeed was that they were able to quickly contact activists around the world to coordinate demonstrations at Bechtel offices. One protest in particular happened to coincide with a big demonstration in Washington against the World Bank and IMF policies. That gave the struggle in Bolivia international publicity. That's real globalization by people, so therefore it's called *antiglobalization*. But it worked.

Rafael Corrêa recently was elected president of Ecuador. What are your thoughts on him?

He's made some interesting comments. There is a big U.S. military base in Ecuador, one of the last big remaining U.S. military bases in South America, and Corrêa was asked during the campaign if he would close it down. He told reporters, "If they let us put a military base in Miami . . . we'll accept" a base in Ecuador.[12] That's a good answer, a reasonable answer.

Mexico had an election in September. Felipe Calderón was elected. The defeated candidate, the former mayor of Mexico City, Andrés Manuel Lopez Obrador, claimed the election was a fraud.[13] Do you think he's right?

The country was split roughly 50–50, so maybe Lopez Obrador is right about the fraud. In fact, there is some evidence for it. But as far as the character of the country is concerned, it doesn't matter much if the election went one way or the other. There are huge problems all over the country. That's why the United States is building a wall along its border with Mexico, to contain the problems they anticipate getting worse.

The wall is an atrocity. If you take a look at the Mexican border, it was once pretty open, porous in both directions. Then Clinton militarized the border for the first time with Operation Gatekeeper in 1994. Now the militarization is getting more intense. Why 1994? That was the year when the North American Free Trade Agreement (NAFTA) was passed. And presumably the United States expected that the effect of NAFTA would be that Mexican agriculture could not compete with highly subsidized U.S. agribusiness exports, so people would flock to the cities. Domestic Mexican businesses would not be able to compete with U.S. multinationals, which receive special treatment in Mexico under mislabeled trade laws that have little to do with trade but are about ensuring investor rights. The result would be a flood of people north into the United States, joined by a flood of people leaving the ruins of Central America after Reagan's terrorist wars. So, you build a wall.

Muhammad Yunus of Bangladesh was awarded the 2006 Nobel Peace Prize.[14] He started the Grameen Bank in that country. It's based on microcredit loans to mostly poor women in rural areas. People are always asked, if you don't like capitalism, what about some kind of alternative? Is this perhaps the basis of an alternative?

It's a sensible device. It's not the answer to everything. Empowering women is extremely important in third world countries—actually, in most communities. One of the things that is very noticeable in communities that have been crushed and are barely surviving is that the women seem much more able to do things than men are. And you can see why. The women's responsibilities continue no matter how rotten the situation. They're still taking care of the children, doing all the housework, cooking. Often men, when their usual opportunities are gone, are lost. They have nothing to do. They turn to drink, to crime. You see it all over the place.

So giving microcredit loans to women is a very smart thing to do. It's not the end of everything, but it has paid off. It's a good capitalist approach. This is pure capitalism, actually, much purer than the U.S. economy. It's real capitalism. The U.S. economy is state-based to a large extent.

The current pope, Benedict XVI, who has managed to mire himself in controversy around his statements about Islam, was known as the enforcer during the reign of the much revered and hallowed Pope John Paul II.[15] *He was the guy who apparently purged high-ranking Catholic officials who supported liberation theology.*

We don't know the inner workings of the Vatican, but that's been reported. And it certainly looks like that from his writings. The crime of liberation theology was that it takes the Gospels seriously. That's unacceptable. The Gospels are radical pacifist material, if you take a look at them. When the Roman emperor Constantine adopted Christianity, he shifted it from a radical pacifist religion to the religion of the Roman Empire. So the cross, which was the symbol of the suffering of the poor, was put on the shield of the Roman soldiers. Since that time, the Church has been pretty much the church of the rich and the powerful—the opposite of the message of the Gospels. Liberation theology, in Brazil particularly, brought the actual Gospels to peasants. They said, let's read what the Gospels say, and try to act on the principles they describe. That was the major crime that set off the Reagan wars of terror and Vatican repression. The United States was virtually at war with the Catholic Church in the 1980s. It was a clash of civilizations, if you like: the United States versus the Gospels.

Among liberal opinion there is now tremendous opposition to the Iraq war—

I don't agree with you.

Why?

What's the opposition?

That the occupation hasn't gone well.

But what are they proposing? That it go well. You could have found the same views in Russia during the occupation of Afghanistan. Actually, there was a very interesting article recently in the *Toronto Globe and Mail* by a former Russian soldier who is now a Canadian citizen.[16] He describes how the soldiers felt in Afghanistan. We were trying to help the people of Afghanistan. We were saving them from the terrorists who were attacking them. We were risking our lives to bring them medical care. And somehow they didn't appreciate it. We were trying to protect rights of women and make it a civilized society. He says that he now hears Canadian soldiers saying the same thing about Iraq. You can translate it word for word. I've been in touch with him. This is part of a bigger project comparing the attitudes in Russia toward the Afghan war, the Chechnya war, what appears in the press there and so on, with attitudes here and what appears in the press here about U.S. wars. Pretty much as I expected, it's very similar.

A number of people opposed to the Iraq occupation say they support the invasion and occupation of Afghanistan.

It's true. The Afghan war is supposed to be a good war. First of all, in my view—which is very unpopular, so I'll repeat it—the Afghan war itself was a major war crime.

Explain why. People say, "We were attacked on September 11.

Didn't the terrorists come from Afghanistan? And that's where the Taliban were protecting Al Qaeda."

First of all, we don't even know that the attacks came from Afghanistan. Eight months after the bombing began, the head of the FBI, Robert Mueller, had a big interview with the *Washington Post* in which he was asked what he knew about the September 11 attacks. He said that the idea may have been hatched in Afghanistan, but it was probably implemented in the Gulf Emirates and in Germany.[17] That's what we believed eight months after the attack on Afghanistan began, which means we knew nothing at the time of the bombing. The bombing was not undertaken to get rid of the Taliban. That was an afterthought, added three weeks later. The bombing was undertaken with a very explicit threat: you turn over to us Osama bin Laden or else we'll bomb you. No evidence, no request for extradition. In fact, the Taliban made some gestures—we don't know whether they were serious or not because they were rejected—to hand bin Laden over in an appropriate way, if evidence was given, maybe to a third country.[18] That was just blocked. We're going to bomb.

Were Afghans in favor of it? Many anti-Taliban Afghans bitterly opposed the bombing, including the U.S. favorite, Abdul Haq. About two weeks after the bombing started, he gave a long interview in which he bitterly condemned it.[19] He said that you're bombing and killing Afghans, you're undermining our efforts to overthrow the Taliban from within, which we can achieve, and you're doing it just because you want to show your muscle. A week later, there was a meeting in Peshawar in Pakistan of about a thousand Afghans, many trekking across the border from Afghanistan, some from Pakistan. It was reported. They didn't agree on much, but one thing they agreed on was opposing the bombings.[20]

What's happening in the country now is extremely ugly. It's back in the hands of warlords, the kind of people who terrorized the country so badly that the Taliban were welcomed. It's a major horror. The country is back to living off opium production.[21] However rotten the Taliban were, they stopped that.[22] Nobody wants the Taliban back, but what's happening there is awful.

Michael Walzer has written about Afghanistan as "a triumph of just war theory."[23] You've been a critic of his views.

I haven't been so much a critic of his views as rather an observer of the fact that they are just views. If you look at the book you're quoting from, *Arguing About War*, there are two problems with it. One, there are no arguments— not a single one. The arguments all reduce to: "I believe" or "I think" or "it seems to me." That's not an argument. The second interesting fact is that there are no opponents.

He's giving arguments, but against whom? "Radical pacifists" or "they say on campus" or something like that. This is intellectually deplorable. Actually, he does mention two people. One of them is his major enemy, Edward Said. He makes some outrageous statement in a footnote about people who support terror, saying that's Edward Said's position.[24] And then he says in a more moderate way, this position has been indicated by Richard Falk.[25] Because Falk is more respectable, you've got to be more polite. Walzer's famous book *Just and Unjust Wars* was pretty similar.[26] It's very hard to find an argument. Just "I think." He's repeating conventional wisdom, so you can't really blame him for it. But on what grounds is Afghanistan a triumph of the just war theory?

One of Walzer's colleagues, Jean Bethke Elshtain, wrote an equally horrible book—intellectually outrageous and morally depraved, in my opinion.[27] She says Afghanistan was a triumph of just war theory, and then gives a set of reasons. The trouble is, every single one of her reasons is a complete falsehood. I went through this in print in *Hegemony or Survival*, so I won't repeat myself.[28] But she got the facts wrong, and her arguments don't apply. Some of them are flatly contradicted by what happened, but that doesn't matter. Just war theory has been converted into a form of apologetics for whatever atrocities your favored state is carrying out.

One component of war resistance in the late 1960s and early 1970s was the establishment of GI coffeehouses. The documentary Sir! No Sir! *and the book* Soldiers in Revolt *tell this story.[29] That whole idea is being revived right now. There is one being set up near Fort Drum in upstate New York, where the Tenth Mountain Division is based.[30] Describe the GI coffeehouse movement for those who may not be familiar with it. Was it effective?*

It was a support system for soldiers run by the antiwar movement, and it was very effective. The coffeehouses were located near bases. They were just places for soldiers to come. They could do whatever they wanted. Nobody was trying to propagandize them. There were discussion groups, and if they wanted to join them, fine. Some of the discussion groups were organized by the antiwar activists who set the coffeehouses, but the soldiers made the decisions. This had an effect in building up what was a very significant movement. There were also war crimes trials run by GIs where soldiers and officers reported on what they had done and what they had witnessed in Vietnam.

There were a series of them around the country, and they were very effective.[31] I think this is a good time to renew that.

David Krieger directs the Nuclear Age Peace Foundation in Santa Barbara. In a recent article, he asked the question, "Why are there still nuclear weapons?" And he proposes some answers.[32] What would you say?

Simply that the nuclear-armed states are criminal states. They have a legal obligation, confirmed by the World Court, to live up to Article 6 of the Nuclear Non-Proliferation Treaty (NPT), which calls on them to carry out good-faith negotiations to eliminate nuclear weapons entirely. None of the nuclear states has lived up to it. The United States has violated the agreement much more than others. It's in the lead in violating the NPT—especially this administration, which has stated that it isn't subject to Article 6 and has developed new nuclear weapons systems.[33] The Non-Proliferation Treaty is just one of a collection of treaties. The others have been dismantled and blocked by the Bush administration. In fact, the United States just entered into an agreement with India, ratified by Congress, that tears to shreds the central part of the Non-Proliferation Treaty.[34]

India is not even a signatory of the NPT.

India is not a signatory, and it developed nuclear weapons on its own, which is a real crime.

Like Pakistan and Israel.

Like Pakistan and Israel. Of course, developing weapons outside the treaty is worse than what Iran is doing. And the Bush administration has effectively endorsed it, which, as Gary Milhollin, one of the main specialists on nuclear weapons, correctly pointed out in an article in *Current*

History, tears the core of the treaty apart.[35] If the United States can do these deals, why can't everybody else? And sure enough, China approached India with a similar deal and also approached Pakistan.[36] Once you set the precedent, the most powerful state in the world, others are going to follow.

This is not a joke. The threat of nuclear war is extremely serious and is growing, and part of the reason is that the nuclear states, led by the United States, simply refuse to live up to their obligations, or are significantly violating them.

THE FRAMEWORK FOR THINKABLE THOUGHTS

CAMBRIDGE, MASSACHUSETTS (JANUARY 29, 2007)

How is fighting power today different from in the 1960s and the early 1970s?

Right now, it's a lot easier than the early 1960s. At that point, it was extremely hard to do anything even mildly critical of state power. You could protest racist sheriffs in Alabama, but nothing much in the North—and certainly not the Vietnam War. Antiwar protests didn't really develop even to the level of the protests against the United States invasion of Iraq today. So, in that respect, things have changed.

There are many topics that were almost unmentionable then that you can talk about quite freely and openly now, without any holds barred. After 1967, for example, the issue of Israel became kind of holy writ. You couldn't say a word against it. In fact, that lasted for a long time. But in the last few years, that's eased up, too. You can now talk pretty freely about Israel without hysteria— meetings being broken up, police protection, and so on. Also, environmental issues, women's rights, a number of subjects you can talk freely about now, just weren't even discussed. Solidarity movements didn't exist. By now, there are almost no issues that are so far off the agenda that you can't discuss them, including the nature of the state capitalist system. For example, the idea that there could be an anticorporate movement was almost unimaginable in the 1960s. Now people understand what you're talking about. There are movements, there are recognizable attempts to eliminate the illegitimacy of private tyrannies.

What about discussions of imperialism?

The same thing. Now it's open. If you want to talk about imperialism, it's fine. The only questions that come up are about what is exactly the right concept to use. In the 1960s, you simply couldn't raise questions about the fundamental benevolence of U.S. policy. First of all, there was a John F. Kennedy cult. Take someone like Eugene McCarthy, who was considered a hero in the 1960s. By today's standards, he would be regarded as a charlatan. Here's a guy who did absolutely nothing. In 1968, when it looked like there was an opportunity, he appeared on the stage, and without saying very much managed to mobilize a lot of young people who wanted to seriously change things. The "Clean for Gene" crowd came to Chicago and were beaten bloody on the streets, and McCarthy didn't do anything about it. And as soon as he lost his chance to gain political power, he basically disappeared. Instead of using the prestige he had, even if illegitimately, he went off to write about baseball, make clever remarks, and write poetry. I don't think somebody could get away with that today.

What are the weaknesses and fissures that can be exploited and opened wider in terms of power?

Right now the major fissure to exploit is the basic split in the country between the public and the country's real power sectors. Both of the political parties and the business sector are well to the right of the population on a host of major issues. That's significant. You see these fissures everywhere.

There is a lot of talk right now about how the United States is a divided country. We have to bring it together, "red states" and "blue states." In fact, it is a divided country, but not in the way that's being discussed. It's divided between the public and the power systems, the government and the corporate system. We see it every day. Take the next major issue coming up—Iran. The overwhelming majority of the population is in favor of diplomatic initiatives rather than confrontation.[1] But U.S. public opinion doesn't count, just as Iraqi public opinion doesn't count.

Or take the Iraq Study Group report.[2] It's quite interesting to read, but it is mostly interesting for what it doesn't say. One of the things the report doesn't say is what the population of Iraq wants. That's never mentioned. Actually, they cite the U.S. government and other Western polls that correctly show the proportion of Iraqis who think it's legitimate to attack U.S. soldiers is now 61 percent, but not the figures from the same polling about the percentage of Iraqis who also want the United States to leave.[3] And the report's conclusion is that we have to adjust our tactics so Iraqis don't see us as occupiers. Those very same polls say that in Baghdad two-thirds of the population wants the U.S. troops out immediately and the large majority in the country as a whole wants a firm timetable for withdrawal in a year or less, maybe six months to a year.[4] That's what the Iraqi people want, according to Western polls. That's not mentioned.

You're of that generation that remembers when there was a lively union movement in this country. The percentage of organized workers in the private sector today is at a record low, and it's only slightly better in the public sector.[5] What's the possibility of reviving the union movement, and what needs to be done to make that happen?

What you say is quite true. Actually, public sector unionization has stayed pretty steady, which illustrates the fact, as we know from other sources, that workers would join unions if they could.[6] In the public sector, there are rules that make it difficult to employ illegal measures to block unionization. In the private sector, since Ronald Reagan, the government has made it explicit that employers can use illegal measures to undermine union organizing, and it's done constantly.[7] There have been other changes in the international economy that affect unionization. Can this be reversed? It certainly can. But it's going to mean overcoming a lot of pressures. There are no new secrets about this. The methods of organizing are known. They just have to be pursued. And it's not something that can be done only by working people. It means making changes in the cultural background and other kinds of organization—support and solidarity and so on.

The U.S. economy is fairly stagnant and is laden with deficits and debt. The manufacturing base is eroding. What do you see as the future of the economy?

I don't think anybody really knows. It's a kind of economy that never existed before. Take, say, the auto industry. If by the "United States" you mean the territorial United States, then the manufacturing base is declining. But if you mean the people who *own* the United States, then it's not declining. U.S.-based multinationals just happen to be producing or assembling cars abroad.

Is it fair to call them the ruling class?

Yes. We can call them the owners of the society, who pretty much run the government, too. They're doing fine. I haven't seen the latest statistics, but their share of global manufacturing has remained quite high over a long period. If you were to take imports to the United States that are coming from affiliates or subsidiaries of U.S. corporations abroad, and count them as domestic production, the trade deficit would sharply decline. And that makes sense. These are imports only in the sense in which some movement across borders within a command economy is trade. But it's a difficult situation. The country is deeply in debt, there are enormous trade deficits, households are deeply in debt, there is great corporate debt.

Savings are negative.

The recent few years have been the first ones of negative savings.[8] A lot of personal wealth is in the form of home ownership, which is a pretty fragile base. There is good evidence to think that there is a housing bubble that somehow overcame the collapse of the stock bubble. If the housing bubble bursts, it could turn out to be very serious. In fact, the housing market is already declining.

Another real risk is that substantial holders of U.S. debt—particularly China, but also Japan—might decide to diversify their currency holdings.

China owns about one trillion dollars of the U.S. debt.[9] What if the Chinese decide to cash in their chips?

I think it's unlikely. China has a lot invested, for example, in U.S. Treasury bonds, which are not a great investment. They could have more profitable investments elsewhere. Holding the dollar is not particularly profitable either, because it's declining relative to the euro. China is consciously propping up the U.S. economy. The United States is their major market, so they want to maintain it for their exports. In order to do that, they have to lose money on the holding of currency and on investments here. At some point, they may change their minds, but that would be a big change in the international economy. I don't think anyone can predict what the effect would be.

There has been talk of Venezuela and Iran pricing their oil sales in euros. How do the owners benefit from the pricing of oil sales in dollars? What are the economic implications if there is a shift to the euro?

When your own currency is effectively the international currency, you have a number of advantages. You don't have to buy the international currency, for example. You've got it. If the Treasury Department wants to adjust the level of the dollar relative to other currencies, it can do it on the basis of profitability for dollar holders, meaning ourselves. Others have to compensate.

From what I read of the international economics literature, I don't think it's at all clear how much of an effect there would be if there were a diversification into euros or Japanese yen, or a broader basket of currencies. As far as I can see, it's quite hard to predict. Very likely there would be some kind of harmful effect for the U.S. economy. What the scale would be is hard to judge. Remember, the United States is a very powerful society. It's still by far the richest country in the world. It has enormous advantages. If you compare it to, say, the entire European Union, it's more or less on a par economically. But this is a single country. It's internally much more integrated than the European Union is.

There has been an upsurge in bellicose language toward Iran. Under the UN Charter, not just the use of force but the threat of force is a breach of the charter.

Article 2 outlaws the threat or use of force in international affairs. But the United States is an outlaw state, and it is accepted by the intellectual class here that it should be an outlaw state, so it is not subject to international law and norms. There is no criticism of this. The only criticism is that maybe these threats will get us into trouble—not that we are committing a crime.

We can say the same about the invasion of Iraq. There is a huge debate about the invasion of Iraq, but no question about whether we have a justification to do it. Of course, we have an automatic justification to do it—because it's us. We have a justification to do anything. In fact, if you look at the so-called debate about Iraq, it's at approximately the level of a high school newspaper commenting on the local sports team. You don't ask whether the team has a right to win, you just ask how they can win. Do we need a new coach? Do we have too many injuries? Should we try some new tactics? But not, do we have a right to win? It's an unthinkable thought. The question of whether the United States has a right to win in Iraq is unthinkable. Of course it does. Everyone is in favor of victory. The only question is whether this strategy or the other strategy will produce it.

Some of the discussion that's going on is almost surreal. For example, a couple of days ago it was announced that Iran is opening a bank in Iraq.[10] There was a huge furor about how this proves Iranian interference in Iraq. You don't know whether to laugh or cry. Suppose Russia in the 1980s had protested because the United States was opening a bank in Afghanistan, saying, "You're interfering with our liberation of Afghanistan." People would have collapsed in hysterical laughter. But when we say this about Iran, it's correct. We've come close to threatening that we might have a right to attack Iran if there is Iranian interference in Iraq.[11] The comparison isn't fair to Russia, but it's as if the Russians had claimed the right to bomb the United States in the 1980s because we were interfering in Afghanistan, which we certainly were. We were supporting major terrorist forces in Afghanistan.

Many people don't think that the United States will attack Iran. The military is overextended, there is no popular support for it. But when Richard Nixon inherited the Vietnam War, instead of ending it he expanded it into Cambodia and Laos. Are people expecting rational behavior from irrational actors?

First of all, extending the war to Cambodia and Laos was horrible enough, but it was basically costless to the United States. You're attacking countries that are totally defenseless. The only issue was domestic opposition and international protest. If you attack Iran, it can blow up the whole region. It's a serious war. So I don't think the comparison to Nixon is fair to Nixon. And many comparisons to Nixon are unfair. Even domestically, he was more or less the last liberal president.

There was a lot of protest around the Cambodian invasion.

When the United States invaded Cambodia in 1970, then there was protest, because people didn't want an expansion of the war. In fact, there was enough protest that

Congress finally barred the official U.S. bombing campaign there. The actual bombing continued, though there was very little reporting of it.[12] It was not a mainstream issue. When the issue of the possible impeachment of Nixon came up, the Cambodia bombing—which was illegal and in violation of congressional legislation—was raised, but it was taken off the bill of indictment.[13] It wasn't that important.

Just a couple of years ago, the Clinton administration released documents on the bombing of Cambodia. And it turns out the tonnage of bombing was nearly five times as high as the very high level that had previously been known.[14] People have speculated that the bombing must have played a role in the formation of the Khmer Rouge, but now, from the documentation that's been released, it's almost obvious. This meant that Cambodia was the most heavily bombed country in history. It's public. There was an article about this by one of the leading Cambodia specialists, Ben Kiernan. He's the head of the Yale University Cambodian Genocide Project, which is mostly focused on Pol Pot's genocide but extends beyond. The article appeared in a small Canadian journal.[15] It was published at least once in the United States, on ZNet.[16] As far as I'm aware, that's the first publication in the United States.

During the period of the bombing, the Khmer Rouge grew from maybe ten thousand to a couple hundred thousand.[17] They were surely using the bombing, which was driving peasants berserk, as a mobilizing technique.

So, here's information of enormous significance about the bombing of Cambodia, but there was no interest. Then, sometimes things are published that are utterly shocking but pass without comment, like Nixon and Kissinger's orders in December 1970 for "a massive bombing campaign in Cambodia . . . [using] anything that flies on anything that moves."[18] If we found a statement like that in the Serbian archives about Milošević, it would be reported with banner headlines. Here is a call for genocide, basically, in the *New York Times* with no comment. The whole history of the Indochina wars has been so reshaped that it's unrecognizable. By now people have no idea what happened. You can see that in the comparisons that are drawn between Vietnam and Iraq. There is almost no meaningful comparison, either in the motives, the character of the war, or in the way the war ended. The similarities are almost nonexistent.

Frank Rich of the New York Times *believes that "the Iraq-Vietnam parallels at this juncture are striking."*[19]

Yes, but these are superficialities. Vietnam was fought for totally different reasons. And by about 1970, the United States had effectively won its major war aims—to destroy the country and ensure that the region was inoculated from "infection," to use the government's terms. But you can't destroy Iraq and inoculate the region from the threat of successful development. That's totally irrelevant in Iraq. In order to see that, though, you have to be willing to face the facts about why the United States invaded South Vietnam and why it invaded Iraq—and why it's almost unthinkable for them to leave Iraq.

In discussions on Iran, you often hear tropes from the Munich narrative—appeasement, Hitler, Nazi Germany. You have CNN's Glenn Beck saying, "Iran is a global threat as big as what we've seen since the Nazis."[20] Why is this story recycled so often? And why do people seemingly fall for it?

I presume the people who are producing this rhetoric fall for it. I don't see any particular reason to think they're lying, but it's so utterly outlandish, it's hard even to comment on. First of all, Munich was welcomed by the Roosevelt administration. Sumner Welles, Roosevelt's main adviser, came back glowing with praise for what had been accomplished. They had established peace in Europe forever. The business community in the United States, and even more so in England, were fairly supportive of Hitler. After Hitler came to power, investment in Germany shot up. Now that's all gone from history. One part of the story is true, though. If the United States and Britain had wanted to stop Hitler in 1938, they probably could have done it. There wouldn't have been any war, but they didn't particularly want to.

Or in 1937 or 1936?

In earlier years, almost certainly. But even as late as 1938, it probably would have still been possible to end the threat of war. By 1939, Germany was a major military power, and came very close to conquering Europe.

Iran, in stark contrast, wasn't able to defeat Iraq in the 1980s. By now, its military force is almost nonexistent. It can barely hold the country together. Has Iran ever threatened anyone? Has it attacked anyone? It wouldn't have the military force to do it. You can say what you like about Iran: it has a horrible government. We obviously don't want them to have nuclear weapons. But to consider them a threat comparable to Hitler kind of reminds me of when Ronald Reagan put on his cowboy boots and declared that we have to have a national emergency because the Nicaraguan army is "just two days' drive from Harlingen, Texas."[21]

No one wants Iran to have nuclear weapons. If you're serious about this, though, there are ways of dealing with the problem sensibly. To regard Iran as a serious threat, let alone a threat comparable to Hitler, that's to move into outer space. You can't discuss it rationally. It's like talking to a religious fanatic.

Benjamin Netanyahu says, "It's 1938 and Iran is Germany."[22]

He has his reasons. Israel recognizes that there is a threat—namely, that Iran is a threat to its regional dominance. Israel wants to dominate the region completely, with no competing forces, and Iran might be some slight counterbalance. But it's not a serious threat to them. From a military point of view, almost surely not. Suppose Iran had nuclear weapons. Could they use them? If there were even the slightest indication that Iran is planning to arm a missile, the country would be vaporized. The only thing they can use nuclear weapons for is as a deterrent. They can't attack anyone with nuclear weapons unless they decide on mass suicide.

You could argue that maybe they'll leak weapons to terrorists. That's conceivable. But then there is a much more serious threat of that right in front of us, Pakistan, which has leaked nuclear weapons.[23] You want to worry about that? Fine. Let's bomb Pakistan.

A little earlier you said that if the United States were to attack Iran, it could lead to a serious conflagration in the Middle East, but you've also said Iran is very weak in comparison to Nazi Germany in 1938.

You don't have to be very strong to stir up the Shiite forces in Iraq and turn the place into a bloodbath, to bring in Saudi Arabian intervention in support of the Sunnis, and so on. That doesn't take military power.

Mohamed ElBaradei, the head of the International Atomic Energy Commission, says he's worried that further UN sanctions against Iran "is only going to lead to an escalation," and then

*he dismissed as "absolutely bonkers" the idea that Israel or the
United States might launch military attacks on Iranian nuclear
sites. Such an attack "would only strengthen the hand of hard-
liners" in Iran, driving its nuclear program underground.[24]*

It would almost certainly. Let's remember what happened
at Osirak, when Israel bombed the Iraqi nuclear facilities
in 1981. It didn't terminate nuclear weapons development. It didn't even accelerate it. It *initiated* it. The Osirak
reactor was inspected within weeks after the bombing, by
the chairman of Harvard's physics department, who is a
specialist in nuclear engineering. He wrote an article in
the world's leading scientific journal, *Nature*, in which he
said that the reactor was not capable of weapons production.[25] From testimony that we now have from Iraqi de-
fectors, it turns out he was apparently correct. The reactor
was not intended for weapons production. But of course
as soon as it was bombed, Saddam Hussein immediately
undertook a clandestine nuclear weapons development
program. So it appears from what we know that the Israeli bombing initiated Iraq's nuclear weapons development program. Something similar could happen in Iran,
too. I would be really surprised if there isn't an office in
the Pentagon that's thinking through contingency plans
about how to take over Khuzestan, the Arab region of
Iran right near the Gulf, which happens to be where most
of the country's oil is, and just bomb the rest of the country to dust.

Who knows what effect that would have on the world? Hatred and fear of the United States and Israel would escalate to an immeasurable degree. It's already huge. So, in that sense, any use of military force would be crazy. We know from polls in the region that the populations in the surrounding countries, who very much dislike Iran—Turkey, Saudi Arabia, Pakistan—nevertheless by large majorities prefer a nuclear-armed Iran to any form of military action.[26] Though the next to last thing in the world they want is a nuclear-armed Iran, the last thing they want is military action. And what would that lead to? It's a question of the extent to which you can control populations by force, violence, and threat. Maybe you can. It's been done in the past. But it's a terrible gamble.

The Bush administration accuses Iran of "meddling" in Iraq. There is no sense of irony here.

Yes, but that's standard. During the Vietnam War, for example, when the United States was bombing North Vietnam, it happened to be bombing an internal Chinese railroad. The way the French built railroads, the internal Chinese railroads from southwest to southeast China pass through North Vietnam. When China sent in workers to rebuild the bombed railroad, that was condemned as interference in Vietnam. For us to bomb is legitimate. For them to repair their railroad that we're bombing shows that they are aggressors, and therefore we have to think about bombing China, and so on.

These formulations have a lot of significance. If you can get people to repeat without ridicule that Iran is interfering in Iraq or that China is interfering in Vietnam, it entrenches the fundamental principle that we have a right to use violence anywhere we like and nobody has a right to deter it. No one. That's an important principle.

In your book On Power and Ideology, *you wrote, "One of the most effective devices is to encourage debate, but within a system of unspoken presuppositions that incorporate the basic principles of the doctrinal systems. These principles are therefore removed from inspection; they become the framework for thinkable thought, not objects of rational consideration."*[27]

Exactly. And the presuppositions become so deeply entrenched that you can't see them. So even to ask the question of whether the United States has the right to win in Iraq, it's as if you're speaking Swahili. It doesn't have any meaning in the English language. Devices such as charging China with meddling in Vietnam or Iran with meddling in Iraq help serve that function. But they have other functions, too. The constant illegal threats against Iran also have the effect of making the leadership in Iran harsher and more repressive. The United States thinks that's a good thing, too, because that might help generate protest, dissension, internal ruptures. I'm sure the United

States is trying to stimulate secessionist movements. Iran is a complicated country. Much of it is non-Persian. It's multilingual, multiethnic. There is a big Azeri population, which is repressed and probably is being stimulated to rebellion, as I mentioned.[28] The United States is probably doing the same in Khuzestan and elsewhere. If the regime becomes harsher and more repressive, it's possible that this may well stimulate other forms of disruption and resistance that will help erode the country from within. That's surely a goal of the United States and Israel. They do not want an independent, stable, powerful Iran, or anyone else that's out of control. But that's quite different from saying the country is a threat.

And it's not just Iran. It's true for the rest of the region, too. You can't mention Hezbollah without saying "Iranian-backed Hezbollah." "Iranian-backed Hamas." You don't talk about "U.S.-backed forces." The U.S.-backed forces are the "moderates," so you don't have to say "U.S.-backed." All of this is a form of demonization constructed to give a justification for the use of violence and terror. And like all propaganda, even the craziest propaganda, there is an element of truth to it. You can't pull propaganda out of the air. It has to have at least some element of credibility. And then if people question the propaganda, they can be bitterly accused of denying what's true.

So if you question the use of these methods of demonization of Iran, the immediate reaction from the intellectual class is that "you're supporting Ahmadinejad. You're a Holocaust denier." That's a useful technique. It's extremely important to protect the right to lie. For intellectuals particularly, that has a very high value. You must protect the right to lie in support of power. And one of the ways of doing it is by participating in the demonization of an enemy. That's standard.

I want to talk a bit about National Public Radio. On January 26, Morning Edition anchor Steve Inskeep called the Golan Heights "a disputed piece of territory between the two countries," Syria and Israel.[29]

That shows how far the distortions have gone. The Israeli annexation of the Golan Heights in December 1981 was bitterly condemned at the time. A unanimous Security Council resolution condemned it.[30] But now the Golan Heights is "disputed." That's the steady, slow erosion that takes place when you keep repeating lies and fabrications, doing your duty of service to power. The United States basically supports the annexation, so therefore it's legitimate.

The same with the Israeli-occupied territories. They're now "disputed." What makes them disputed? It's a purely illegal occupation, and everything that's happening there is in violation of international law, but it's "disputed." The wall through the occupied territories is now regularly described as a "security barrier." It's not a security barrier. It's a security barrier for the settlers. If they wanted a security barrier for Israel, they would build it right inside Israeli territory. Then you can be as secure as you like. You can make it a mile high and have it patrolled on both sides with tanks, so nobody can get through. This is an annexation wall. It was never a security barrier, except for the settlers, who are there illegally.

Furthermore, there is unanimity on that, in the judicial world at least. The World Court advisory opinion on the wall condemned it as illegal. The U.S. justice Thomas Buergenthal, who issued a separate opinion, disagreed with the majority on technical grounds, but agreed with them that the Geneva Conventions apply to the occupied territories, which means any transfer of population there is in violation of international law. And he said that any part of the wall that is protecting settlers—meaning that it is going through the West Bank, as most of it does—is "*ipso facto* in violation of international humanitarian law."[31]

By now it is openly an annexation wall. But step by step people accept more and more state propaganda, they internalize it, and it becomes the basis for the next discussion.

The Israeli narrative completely overwhelms the Palestinian narrative in U.S. discourse.

The point of view of the Palestinians cannot be represented here, or of any other people where the United States is supporting their repression, occupation, and destruction.

It's always puzzled me that even on the left, people, yourself, have not used the term "colonies" and "colonization" and "colonists" to describe what's happening in the West Bank. It might give some clarification. "Settlers" sounds almost innocuous.

I don't use the word *colonization* because it understates the case. It's annexation. We don't talk about the United States colonizing the Southwest. It annexed it. It fought a war, took over half of Mexico, and annexed it. And the United States uses its resources. A lot of the wealth of the Southwest comes from the Mexicans. That's not colonization. It's *conquest*. In the occupied territories, it's a matter of slow conquest, takeover, and annexation. So I don't think *colonization* is the right term for it.

Renée Montagne, who is another Morning Edition *anchor, had a tribute to Teddy Kollek, the longtime Israeli mayor of Jerusalem, who died in early January. She said in her tribute, "He presided over the reunification of the city, tearing down the stone wall that cut across it. . . . He will be remembered as that rare leader who was also a great unifier."[32]*

Teddy Kollek will be remembered by Palestinians as the great leader who was very clear and explicit that he would do nothing for the Palestinians at all unless it was for the benefit of the Jews. He said he had "nurtured nothing and built nothing" for Palestinians in Jerusalem, apart from a sewage system, which was justified on the grounds that if Palestinians had cholera, it might spread to the Jewish areas.[33] But he made it very clear that he was going to do nothing for the Palestinians who were illegally taken over in a city that was illegally annexed and illegally expanded.

As far back as 1968, the Security Council condemned Israel for taking any steps that changed the status of Jerusalem.[34] Step by step, Israel has not only changed its status but, under Kollek in particular, reduced the options of existence for the Palestinian population to a minimum. They don't have building permits, their lands are being taken, they are driven into smaller and smaller areas. Their economic viability is being destroyed. Surrounding areas are being cut off. Kollek was very proudly carrying out these policies. That's why he's called a great unifier.

Juan Williams, who also doubles as a Fox News commentator, is a senior correspondent at National Public Radio. He interviewed George Bush on January 29. In one of his questions, he said to the president, "You know, people are praying for you. . . . The American people want to be with you, Mr. President."[35] The tone of language here is interesting.

It's what you would expect from a very loyal commissar in Stalinist Russia. We want to get behind you, genius Stalin. We want to support you. Please make it easier for us to support you. I don't want to draw the comparison too closely because it's unfair to the Stalinist commissars—they could at least plead fear in extenuation. In a free country, though, you can't plead fear, just cowardice and subordination to power. Why do we want to get behind the president if he's carrying out murderous, violent criminal acts? Why do we want to get behind the president when what he's doing is strongly opposed by the overwhelming majority of the population that he invaded?

There is also very little discussion in the press about the U.S. military bases in Iraq.

It's interesting. There is a line in the Iraq Study Group report saying that the president should inform Iraqis that we don't intend to build permanent military bases.[36] Is there a line in the report saying that we should stop building permanent military bases? No. Just that we should inform people in Iraq that we're not going to do it, but meanwhile keep doing it. They mention in the report that the United States is building an enormous embassy in Baghdad, and it is. It's building a city inside Baghdad, which is self-contained, with its own energy and water and everything else.

It's the biggest U.S. embassy in the world.[37]

Yes, but that's misleading, because it's qualitatively different from any embassy in the world. Did the Iraq Study

Group report say you should stop building it? Did they say that building that city inside Baghdad—and apparently permanent military bases—indicates something about our intentions to withdraw? No. That isn't discussed. Did they discuss the reasons why the United States, including the opposition, is unwilling to withdraw? You can't. These are not sentences in English. In a really well indoctrinated society, you cannot consider unthinkable thoughts.

A French revolutionary, said, "The great are only great because we are on our knees."[38]

That's quite true. If you don't have sycophantic attitudes toward the president—if you don't say, "We're praying for you" and "We want to support you"—they don't look great. A lot of the media are not sycophantic toward Bush. They're pretty bitter, to an extent that's very unusual with regard to a president. That's been true, incidentally, right through the Bush years. He has been under unprecedented attack from the midst of the establishment because the positions of the Bush administration are so far to the extreme of the very narrow spectrum that they are considered harmful to mainstream interests. Before the invasion of Iraq, when Bush announced his National Security Strategy in September 2002, which was in effect an announcement of the potential invasion of Iraq, there was a very strong establishment opposition to it.[39] Within a couple of weeks, *Foreign Affairs* had a major article by a mainstream historian, John Ikenberry, condemning what he called "the new imperial grand strategy" of the Bush administration and saying it's going to be harmful to the United States.[40] *Foreign Policy*, the other major foreign affairs journal, also had articles criticizing Bush.

Yes, but most of the media are echo chambers for the war on Iraq.

That's true for the war on Iraq, but the point is that there was unprecedented establishment critique. You didn't find that in the past. Those are changes. I don't say it's wonderful. When the media had to go along, they went along. So if you watched BBC or CNN when the war started, it was like cheerleading and continued that way. But not like it was in the past. Change comes slowly, but it's there.

INVASIONS AND EVASIONS

CAMBRIDGE, MASSACHUSETTS (FEBRUARY 2, 2007)

I want to ask you about tinkerers versus overhaulers, reforms—cosmetic improvements and adjustments to the system—versus substantive structural change.

There is certainly a difference, but I don't exactly know what the issue is. We should be in favor of both. Sometimes tinkering with the system can be of great help to people. There are some obvious improvements—you could call them tinkering—that could be made with the health care system that would be of enormous benefit.

How about the media, what is called media reform?

It's the same with media reform. If you can induce the media to give somewhat fairer treatment of significant issues through pressure, by competition from alternatives and so on, that's all to the good. It doesn't change anything fundamental, but it can make a difference.

Take, say, right here in Boston, which I've been close to for many years. The main newspaper here is the *Boston Globe*, probably the most liberal newspaper in the country. In the mid-1960s, it was a pretty hawkish, mainstream newspaper. It changed, thanks to the influence of the chief editor, Tom Winship, who I knew pretty well. By the late 1960s, and partly, I think, through the influence of his son, who was a resister—that's how I got to know Tom— the newspaper changed. It was, I think, the first in the country to call for withdrawal of U.S. troops from Vietnam.[1] And through the 1980s it was one of the few newspapers that had some serious coverage of events in Central America, actually describing what was happening.

When Tom Winship retired, his influence waned. The last editor who was within the Winship system was Kirk Scharfenberg, who died in 1992. Since then, the journal has returned pretty much to what it was in the 1960s. They still have some very good correspondents, and you find articles in there that are of interest, but the general tone of the newspaper has changed quite a lot.

Those were modifications due to the rise of, in this case, large-scale and active popular movements, as well as individual decisions by editors. I think the opening up of the *Boston Globe* was very important. And that's tinkering, if you like. It didn't change the corporate structure of the journal, which should be done.

Tinkering, to borrow your word, is a preliminary to large-scale change. There can't be large-scale structural change unless a very substantial part of the population is deeply committed to it. It's going to have to come from the organized efforts of a dedicated population. That won't happen, and shouldn't happen, unless people perceive that the reform efforts, the tinkering, are running into barriers that cannot be overcome without institutional change. Then you get pressure for institutional change. But short of that realization, there is no reason why people should take the risks, make the effort, or face the uncertainty and the punishment that's involved in serious change. That's why every serious revolutionary is a reformist. If you're a serious revolutionary, you don't want a coup. You want changes to come from below, from the organized population. But why should people be willing to undertake what's involved in serious institutional change unless they think that the institutions don't permit them to achieve just and proper goals?

Walter Lippmann wrote, "All the world thinks of the United States today as an empire, except the people of the United States. We shrink from the word 'empire' and insist that it should not be used to describe the dominion we exercise from Alaska to the Philippines, from Cuba to Panama and beyond.

We feel there ought to be some other name for the civilizing work we do so reluctantly in these backward countries." That was 1927. Has anything changed?[2]

First of all, his comment was a bit too narrow. The conquest of the national territory was also effectively imperialism. If you look at serious historians of imperialism, Bernard Porter, for example, points out that we should not succumb to the "saltwater fallacy," the idea that imperial conquest means crossing a body of saltwater.[3] It can also mean territorial expansion. As he discusses, the territorial expansion of the colonies to what is regarded as the national territory is settler colonialism.[4] It's the form of imperialism in which you actually get rid of the indigenous population and take it over—an extreme form.

The era Lippmann is talking about is the period that began in 1898, when the United States moved toward saltwater imperialism. One can ask how significant a change that was. Certainly it's significant, but how significant? From the point of view of the indigenous population of the United States, it didn't matter much whether we crossed saltwater or not. The same is true for the Mexicans, when we took half of Mexico in a war of conquest one hundred and fifty years ago. But there is a difference. Exactly what name you want to use for it I don't think matters very much. "Empire" is a very ambiguous term, like most terms of political discourse. It's conquest and domination and hegemony.

Another qualification should be added to Lippmann's point. What he's describing, kind of ironically—our spreading of civilized values and so on—is what's usually called "American exceptionalism" in the scholarly and popular literature. The only problem with that is it's not an exception. It's close to universal. I can't think of a dominant conquering power that didn't describe itself in those terms.

Hannah Arendt wrote, "Imperialism would have necessitated the invention of racism as the only possible 'explanation' and excuse for its deeds, even if no race-thinking had ever existed in the civilized world."[5] Does imperialism require racism?

There is a lot of truth to that. Modern racism is to a substantial extent a consequence of imperial conquest. So, for example, if you look back at the intellectual debates in England and France during the Enlightenment, the eighteenth century, there were discussions about whether apes are different from Negroes, whether they're humans, and whether they have language or the capacity for language. In fact, some quite amusing proposals were made. For example, one French thinker suggested that apes are really smarter than humans because they pretend they can't speak.[6] They knew that if they spoke, we would enslave them, just like we enslaved the others who are sort of like them who do speak. This idea may have been jest, but it expressed an uncertainty as to whether other creatures were as noble and advanced as we were, or had human souls, for example.

Yes, a lot of this is the consequence of conquest. When you conquer somebody and suppress them, you have to have a reason. You can't just say, "I'm a son of a bitch and I want to rob them." You have to say it's for their good, they deserve it, or they actually benefit from it. We're helping them. That was the attitude of slave owners. Most of them didn't say, "Look, I'm enslaving these people because I want easily exploitable, cheap labor for my own benefit." They said, "We're doing them a favor. They need it." The anthropologists of the nineteenth century explained that blacks had curved spines because they were genetically adapted to picking cotton.[7] Therefore, we're helping them do what they're good at. Ideas like this go right through the history of imperial conquest. But it took on a particularly virulent form with European imperialism, starting in the seventeenth and eighteenth centuries.

You often cite polls. How do you decide when they are useful? A now infamous Harris poll from late July 2006 found that a full 50 percent of U.S. respondents, up from 36 percent in February 2005, believed that Iraq had weapons of mass destruction.[8] How would you explain this?

Actually, that question has been raised in a number of polls. Harris polls give good information, but they don't go much into the background. You find more detailed information in the studies of the Program of International Policy Attitudes (PIPA) at the University of Maryland. Steven Kull, who directs PIPA, noted that the percentage of the population that continued to believe Iraq had weapons of mass destruction remained fairly steady, even after the government had conceded that there were none.[9] My own feeling is that the reason relates very closely to what we were talking about with regard to imperialism. We invaded Iraq. We don't want to say we're monsters, so we must have had a reason for it. So the reason must have been that they really did have weapons of mass destruction. Yes, somebody in the government made some comment, but I'd rather believe Dick Cheney.

I sense you're somewhat uneasy talking about the so-called Israel lobby in the United States. For a long time, you've said it's a factor influencing U.S. foreign policy but is in no way decisive. Do you still feel that way?

Part of the reason I'm reluctant to talk about this is that it all vastly underestimates the scale and influence of the Israel lobby. Take, say, the outcry over the Rachel Corrie play in New York and elsewhere.[10] That wasn't because of the intervention of the American Israel Public Affairs Committee (AIPAC). That's a reflection of the U.S. intellectual and cultural community.

In New York.

In New York and much of the country. New York happens to be a center. Los Angeles is another. So is Boston. It's fundamentally the intellectual culture, not just AIPAC or the Anti-Defamation League. If you look at the recent paper by John Mearsheimer and Stephen Walt on the Israel lobby, they define it as those sectors that seek to control opinion and attitudes to elicit support for Israeli policies, including aggression, atrocities, and so on.[11] Okay, let's take that definition of the lobby. The main component of it is the U.S. intellectual community and the media. AIPAC doesn't write the editorials of the *New York Times*.

You have to look at the broader intellectual culture. And you can date the beginning of the enthusiastic support for Israel in the culture pretty well, since 1967. Before 1967, the intellectual community was skeptical about Israel or uninterested in it. That changed.

If you look at Norman Podhoretz's book *Making It*, a kind of self-advertisement that came out in 1967, there is barely a mention of Israel.[12] In the mid-1950s, *Commentary*—now a rabid, ultra-extremist Israeli propaganda journal—was considered so critical of Israel the American Jewish Committee created an independent journal called *Midstream* to present the Israeli point of view. Take a look at *Dissent*. They don't like the description, but its support for Israeli crimes is often shocking. Its current issue compares Israel's invasion of Lebanon to our own "misadventure" in Iraq, and laments that "Israel failed to achieve its aims at great cost to Lebanon and to itself."[13]

That's called criticism. But if you look back pre-1967, there was almost nothing on Israel. People writing for *Dissent* regarded Zionism as uninteresting or maybe a nationalist diversion.

So it's your view that after June 1967, U.S. elites saw Israel as a military power that it could use in the Middle East?

From the point of view of the U.S. government, the 1967 war and Israel's huge military success essentially confirmed earlier thoughts that you see in the intelligence record of the National Security Council and other planning institutions.[14] A "logical corollary" of opposition to "radical Arab nationalism," meaning independent Arab nationalism, "would be to support Israel as the only strong pro-West power left in the Near East," and therefore the most reliable base for U.S. power in that part of the world. I'm quoting from documents written in 1958, a very significant year in U.S.-Mideast affairs.[15] Israel was the only country to have participated in the British-American interventions in the region—in Lebanon and Jordan, particularly—to try to prevent the spread of the threat of Iraqi nationalism after the overthrow of the British-backed government in Baghdad in 1958. Israel was the only country that helped out. They allowed overflights and so on, which solidified these earlier proposals about Israel's role as an ally. Back in 1948, the Joint Chiefs of Staff had indicated that Israel was potentially the most powerful military force in the region after Turkey, and that it could be a base for U.S. power.[16]

But 1967 nailed it down. The main importance was that Nasser was destroyed. Nasser was the symbol and the center of secular Arab nationalism. The U.S. government was afraid of what he represented. For one thing, Nasser was fighting a proxy war with Saudi Arabia in Yemen, so he was regarded as a threat to the Saudi monarchy—the oldest and most valued U.S. ally in the region, because that's where the oil is.

Remember, throughout history, the United States has tended to support the most extreme fundamentalist Islamic groups and to oppose secular nationalism. So, Israel smashed Nasser and destroyed the threat of secular nationalism. There was a lingering concern that the Arabs might want to use the wealth of the region for their own population, not for Western wealth and power, with a little bit raked off for the gangsters that run the countries. That's a major threat. Israel finished that, which firmed up the U.S.-Israeli alliance and led to a very quick change.

U.S. aid to Israel skyrocketed.

The aid skyrocketed. But also the attitudes of educated elites toward Israel changed radically. When Israel intervened to prevent a potential Syrian move to protect Palestinians who were being massacred by the Jordanian army during Black September in 1970, U.S. aid to Israel again increased dramatically. And other attitudes changed sharply. That's when you start getting concern about the Holocaust. Before that, when people could have actually done something for Holocaust victims—say, in the late 1940s—they didn't do anything. That changed after 1967. Now you have Holocaust museums all over the country. It's the biggest issue, and you have to study it everywhere, mourn it. But not when you could have done something about it.

There were other factors at play, too. You have to remember what was going on in 1967. First of all, the United States was fighting a war in Vietnam and had not been able to crush Vietnamese resistance. Later, intellectual elites will tell you that they were always against the war, but if you look back at the time, it's not true. I went through a lot of the literature of the Kennedy memoirists and others.[17] People just changed their stories. Arthur Schlesinger, for example, says almost nothing about Vietnam in his almost hour-by-hour account of the Kennedy administration in 1962.[18] It was barely discussed. In his later version, when he reconstructed the history, Vietnam was a major issue.[19] Kennedy was trying to get out of Vietnam, and they were discussing it. Everyone suddenly became a longtime opponent of the war

It's very much like Iraq today. The so-called opponents of the war overwhelmingly are opponents of U.S. failure, not opponents of the war. As Schlesinger put it at the time, when he was criticizing Joseph Alsop, the right-wing supporter of the war in Vietnam, "We all pray that Mr. Alsop will be right" and that the United States will win. And if it does, "we may all be saluting the wisdom and statesmanship of the American government" in winning a victory, even if we turn Vietnam into "a land of ruin and wreck."[20] But Alsop's expectations are probably too hopeful, so therefore we have to oppose the war. That's the kind of opposition there was. Later, when the war became unpopular, it changed.

As an aside, we might notice how little has changed in liberal intellectual ideology. Now, "we all pray" that Mr. Kristol will be right in believing that with more force the United States can win in Iraq, and if he is right, we may all be praising "the wisdom and statesmanship" of the Bush administration in establishing a client state—which we will call independent—in "a land of ruin and wreck." But Kristol is probably too optimistic.

So, we're at a time, 1967, when the intellectual world was pretty much the way Schlesinger described, hoping for victory, deeply concerned that we weren't succeeding in beating up those little yellow bastards. And then Israel came along and showed how to treat third world people properly: you kick them in the face. Israel won a lot of points for that. People were making jokes about sending Moshe Dayan over to Vietnam so we could do it right.

Furthermore, there were things happening inside the United States. This was what is now called the "time of troubles," meaning the time when our society was becoming much more civilized. The women's movement was beginning, the student movement. Students weren't just taking orders. Martin Luther King was beginning to organize a poor people's movement. The people who were supposed to be passive, acquiescent, and obedient were standing up for their rights. That's terrifying. Again, symbolically, Israel showed us how to deal with them. You smash them in the face.

Shortly after this came the Ocean Hill and Brownsville conflict in New York, the struggle between the teachers' unions and the black communities. The teachers' unions were substantially Jewish, members of a poor immigrant community of a generation earlier who had worked themselves up, just like the Irish and others. They had moved into the bureaucracy and the better positions. And now the people down at the bottom were trying to do what they had done thirty years ago—run their own schools, fight for their own rights. And you had a sharp conflict. I can remember relatives in the teachers' union who had been Communists all their lives suddenly becoming ultra-right-wingers because of this. Again, symbolically, Israel showed us how to deal with it.

It also became possible to exploit support for Israel as a weapon to beat the hated New Left. Daniel Berrigan and the young students who were not properly deferential could be condemned as being not properly enthusiastic in their support of Israel. They were mostly dovish

Zionists, which was converted into the charge that they wanted to destroy Israel and implant a bloody dictatorship there. Irving Howe was particularly adept in resorting to this device, though there were others as well. I reviewed a lot of the attacks at the time—an interesting record of deceit in the service of power, and often self-aggrandizement, by now well suppressed.[21]

I think all of this had a dramatic effect. Since then, you have overwhelming distortion of the picture of Israel and of the Israeli-Palestinian conflict. But not because of AIPAC. They're just a small part of it.

Mearsheimer and Walt narrow the focus. They define the lobby properly, but then they narrow the focus to some Jewish organizations. They do point out that the numerically biggest group—and politically most influential, probably—is the right-wing Christian evangelicals. They may be anti-Semites, but they're strongly in support of anything Israel does because that's God's will. But I think the importance of the intellectual community—the media, the journalists, a lot of scholarship, the framework in which people perceive things—is very much underestimated.

AIPAC didn't stop the Rachel Corrie play. Though they would like to, they don't have economic power over the media. Surely they have an influence on Congress, but if you look at their influence on Congress, a lot of it is symbolic. It's very easy for Congress to pass resolutions that they know will not be implemented but will pick up support. Almost annually Congress votes to move the U.S. embassy to Jerusalem.[22] They know it's not going to happen. The consequences would be unacceptable. But they can vote for the bill, announce it on the floor of Congress, and pick up campaign contributions.

Mearsheimer and Walt also say that the pro-Israel lobby—mostly AIPAC and so on—has harmed the national interest of the United States. What does the "national interest" mean? That's a mystical term in what's called "realist international relations theory." The realist tradition, which Mearsheimer and Walt come from, claims that states pursue the national interest. What is the national interest? I think Adam Smith was right when he said that the "national interest" is the interest of the "principal architects" of policy.[23] In his day, it was the merchants and manufacturers. Today, it's multinational corporations and so on. But the realist school doesn't discuss that. Realist international relations theory largely disregards the internal distribution of domestic power.

If we go back to Adam Smith's perspective, there is an easy way of testing Mearsheimer and Walt's thesis that the national interest has been harmed by U.S. policy toward Israel. If Mearsheimer and Walt were right, I would be overjoyed. I wouldn't have to bother writing articles, giving talks, being vilified. I would drop the whole business. I would put on a jacket and a tie, go visit Warren Buffet and the corporate headquarters of Lockheed Martin, Intel, and ExxonMobil, and explain to them patiently that their interests are being harmed by a lobby they can put out of business in thirty seconds with their political clout and economic power. That's the tactical conclusion that should be drawn from the Mearsheimer and Walt discussion. But nobody pursues that tactic, and for a good reason, because Adam Smith was right and the "principal architects" of policy are doing just fine. Just yesterday, for example, ExxonMobil announced the biggest profits of any U.S. corporation in history, beating the record from the year before, which they had also set.[24] Lockheed Martin has got money coming out of its ears. Warren Buffet has just bought up a big industry in Israel. Intel has major facilities there.[25] We can go on through the list. They're doing fine. It's not harming their interest.

I think U.S. policies toward Israel are very harmful to the American people and to future generations. But that's not what determines policy.

A point of clarification. Did you mean to say that Mearsheimer and Walt were underestimating the power of the lobby?

Seriously underestimating the power of the lobby as they define it. And I accept their definition. If we define the lobby as those groups that are attempting to influence opinion, attitude, and policies to support what Israel is doing—occupation, aggression, and so on—then they're underestimating it, because they're omitting its major component, which is the people they meet in the faculty club every day.

Let me make just one more comment about this. Since the goals of the "principal architects of policy" in the United States have conformed pretty closely to Israeli policies after 1967, just as a matter of logic, if we want to estimate the influence of groups like AIPAC and others, we have to look at the cases where those policies diverge. So where does U.S. state policy diverge from Israeli government policy? Those are the cases we should look at to see how influential the lobby is. The cases where they conform don't tell you anything. So you look at the cases where they diverge.

There are cases, and they're interesting. A major one just came up two years ago. Israel is by now kind of like a caricature of the United States in many ways. Many of the features of U.S. society have been taken over and exaggerated in Israel. So it's now to a large extent a highly militarized high-tech society, where the economy is based essentially on export of advanced military armaments. Israel needs markets, and the main market is China. But the United States doesn't want Israel to sell high-tech arms to China. So repeatedly there have been serious conflicts over this. Each time Israel has backed down, and the lobby has been silent. The last major case was in 2005. Israel wanted to repair high-tech antiaircraft missiles it had sold to China.[26] The Israeli government insisted that it wouldn't be pressured on this. It was too important. They are an independent country. But the Bush administration ordered Israel not to do it, and insisted on publicly humiliating them. Washington refused to allow high-level Israeli military officials to visit the United States. Their counterparts here wouldn't talk to them. They forced Israel to fire one of their main officials, and insisted on a public apology. They really dragged them through the mud. Of course, Israel agreed. What can they do? Israel can't face down the United States.

What was particularly interesting was the reaction of the lobby. Try to find it. All of this was barely reported in the United States. The lobby was quiet, whether in the Mearsheimer and Walt definition of the lobby or the intellectuals. They were all quiet because they know better than to confront power. If you can go along with power, that's fine. Then they can be strident and outspoken. But when confronted with real power, they back off. This is not the first time it has happened. It happened with Clinton in connection with Phalcon technology.[27] It has happened repeatedly in the past. One quite important case was in 1993, when Israel and North Korea were close to an agreement that North Korea would end missile exports to the Middle East in return for diplomatic recognition and aid.[28] That's very significant for Israeli security. The Clinton administration blocked it. The lobby, whether in the broad or narrow sense, was silent. I think that's a rather general pattern when Israeli interests conflict with serious U.S. state interests. So when you really run into conflicts, it's pretty clear who wins, and not surprising.

Jimmy Carter's new book is Palestine: Peace Not Apartheid.[29] *In a review in the* Nation, *Henry Siegman writes, "Not the least of the ironies of the controversy generated by Carter's book, or by its title, is that on any day of the week, there appear in virtually all major Israeli newspapers and in its other media far more extreme criticisms of the policies of various Israeli governments than one finds anywhere in the United States. Most of Israel's adversarial editorializing would not be accepted in the op-ed pages of America's leading newspapers."[30] Is Siegman on target with that?*

I think he's purposely exaggerating. It's not every day, but the basic point is correct. So take, say, the word *apartheid*, which drove people berserk. The *Boston Globe* editors bitterly denounced it.[31] You can read the word regularly in the editorials in *Ha'aretz*, in reports of B'Tselem, the main Israeli human rights group, and in commentaries by leading analysts. You can read it in Israel, just not here. People like Meron Benvenisti have been using the term for years. It's kind of common coin, talking about exactly what Carter is talking about, what's happening in the occupied territories. Actually talking about the occupied territories is an underestimate, because to a nontrivial extent apartheid exists within Israel itself—but that topic is untouchable. However, just keeping to the territories, as Carter did, he's describing a system for which "apartheid" may be an underestimate.

Carter's book is relatively free of errors, but there are some. The most serious error is that he buys uncritically the standard line here that Israel's invasion of Lebanon in 1982—the worst atrocity they've carried out, killing some 15,000 to 20,000 people and wrecking much of the country—was a reaction to PLO attacks across the border.[32] That's the standard line here, but it's a total fabrication. The fact of the matter is that Israel was attempting to elicit PLO actions as an excuse for the invasion. There was a cease-fire in place, which the Palestinians observed. Israel didn't. The Israelis kept bombing and attacking. When they couldn't elicit a pretext, they just bombed anyway, inventing one.

If you go back to the Israeli press, they were straight about it at the time, right away. A couple of weeks after the invasion, *Ha'aretz*, the main newspaper, published an article by its leading specialist on the Palestinians, Yehoshua Porath, a scholar who is pretty conservative, in which he pointed out that the reason for the invasion was that Palestinian offers of diplomacy and negotiation were becoming a real embarrassment. As he put it, they were "a veritable catastrophe" for Israel.[33] In order to undercut them, it was necessary to destroy the PLO and try to drive them back to terrorism. Israel doesn't care about

PLO terrorism. But calls for negotiation and diplomacy, that's a real threat. In Israel's main newspaper, Porath openly called the invasion a war for the West Bank. The highest political and military echelon also described it that way. But here's a book that's taken to be critical of Israel and it repeats the absurd propaganda line. It's not surprising when Thomas Friedman writes this, but it is interesting when Carter does.

The hysterical denunciations of Carter also omit the most important part of his book. He is, I believe, the first person in the mainstream to have reported something discussed previously only in dissident circles: that the United States and Israel effectively rejected the "road map" of the Quartet (the United States, European Union, Russia, and the UN). Technically, Israel accepted it, while quietly issuing fourteen "reservations" that eviscerated it, supported by the Bush administration. Carter reports this, and includes the reservations in an appendix.[34] That's quite significant. The road map is supposed to be the heart of U.S. policy—of Bush's "vision," as the media call it.[35] But in reality, U.S.-Israeli policy is that Palestinians must be punished severely for voting the wrong way in a free election until the political organization that gained a plurality of the votes, Hamas, accepts three conditions. It must recognize Israel (or, more absurdly, Israel's abstract "right to exist"), renounce violence, and accept the road map (along with other agreements).

The United States and Israel reject all three. They of course do not recognize Palestine or renounce violence. And they have effectively rejected the road map and other agreements. These matters fall into the undiscussable category, which, I presume, is why the most important part of Carter's book remains unmentioned.

THREATS

Let's start by talking about some threats to the planet. On February 2, the United Nations issued a report saying that it was "unequivocal" that global warming is occurring and is "very likely" the result of human activity. Eleven of the dozen years since 1995 were among the twelve hottest years since 1850, when temperatures were first widely recorded.[1]

That's one threat. The effects of global warming are going to come, but you can mitigate them, adjust to them, and prepare for them. The disaster is not imminent. In the case of nuclear weapons, on the other hand, a disaster is always imminent, and the likelihood of catastrophe is increasing. The *Bulletin of the Atomic Scientists* recently moved its doomsday clock up a couple of minutes to "five minutes to midnight."[2] Even conservatives like George Shultz and Henry Kissinger are warning that the nuclear threat is serious and getting more serious.[3] In part, the threat comes from nuclear proliferation. But a lot of the cause of the proliferation is right here. Washington's bellicose, aggressive militarism is causing proliferation.

Actually, you can read about this on the front page of the *New York Times* today.[4] Intelligence sources are now conceding, a bit evasively, that they "misread" the intelligence about North Korea at the very same moment that they "misread" the intelligence about Iraq. In fact, they are escalating the crisis, leading to North Korea developing a plutonium bomb and missiles. Proliferation is a problem, and it's being instigated by the aggressive militarism of the Bush administration, but the main problem remains the stocks of nuclear weapons in the hands of the Great Powers. What's happening in this area is also largely a consequence of U.S. initiatives.

And there is a third serious problem, which also could be imminent. Avian flu is now essentially uncontrollable. If it makes the small leap to a form that can infect humans, which every scientist thinks it's going to do, avian flu could spread very rapidly and put hundreds of millions of people at severe risk.[5] That requires substantial preparations, first of all, developing vaccines and so on, but also having the infrastructure—hospitals, doctors, supplies—needed to deal with the pandemic. Birds fly all over the place. It's not going to be controllable. It could be extremely serious. And nowhere near enough is being done about it or even talked about except among specialist circles, kind of like global warming twenty years ago. Now at least global warming is sort of in the open. Even the Bush administration doesn't deny it—they just don't do anything about it.

Another issue is the global availability of fresh water.

That's extremely serious. As usual, the poor and oppressed suffer the consequences the most. One of the anticipated effects of global warming—and it's already happening—is melting of ice deposits on mountains, glaciers, and so on. The effect of that could be to turn large areas, including very arable areas such as Pakistan, into deserts.[6] Desertification is extending in the Sahara.[7] And there could be some effects here, too. Even in rich industrial countries, water management is extremely poor. There is tremendous leakage and inefficiency. There are millions of people in the world who don't get drinkable water—probably billions.[8] That has always been a serious problem, and it's now growing. The World Bank has done a couple of studies.[9]

It seems the issues that we're talking about require some kind of global governance rather than individual nations dealing with these problems.

It requires cooperative action. We're not going to have a global government because the Great Powers, including the United States, would never concede any of their sovereignty.

Even if they were threatened with extinction?

That depends very much on whether—let's keep to ourselves—the United States can become a functioning democratic society. It's quite likely that the population would accept a decline of sovereignty, but they don't run the country. There is a huge gap between public opinion and public policy on this issue, too. As far as I know, no pollsters have posed the question in the form that you just did. But for a long time, the general population has been highly supportive of UN initiatives to deal with global problems and even security problems. A majority of the population is even in favor of giving up the United Nations Security Council veto and following the general will.[10] There is not a whisper of that in elite circles or in the political class.

Nevertheless, in terms of long-term survival, even ruling elites have to be concerned about their very viability.

They have short-term perspectives. The people in the Bush administration or at ExxonMobil who are pretending that global warming isn't happening and blocking steps to do anything about it—they have grandchildren, too, who have to survive. But it just isn't a factor in decision making.

ExxonMobil actually has been spending millions of dollars—

To support research to show flaws in the scientific theories.[11] Do they have grandchildren, those CEOs? It's not that they're bad people, it's that their institutional role—in fact, their legal obligation—is to make short-term profit and gain short-term market share.

Nevertheless, it would seem that there would be some concern about preserving their own institutions.

Look at automobile companies. They're now going into decline, maybe terminal decline, in the United States. They knew about what was happening decades ago and didn't prepare for it because they're interested in short-term profit and market share. They knew that huge, overpowered, heavy vehicles weren't going to last because of the energy crisis, pollution, and congestion, but they could make short-term profit. In the longer term, they're being pushed out of business. They probably would have been put out of business in the 1980s if the Reagan administration, which was the most protectionist in postwar history, hadn't virtually doubled protectionist measures to try to allow the automotive, steel, and other industries to overcome huge management failures and reconstitute themselves in the face of superior Japanese competition.

Or take, say, Britain, the major great power that preceded the United States, though never on the same scale. Britain talked about free trade in the late nineteenth century when they were so far ahead of the rest of the world in industrialization that British manufacturers assumed they could win in any competition. They were happy to briefly and selectively level the playing field, but with plenty of constraints. For example, they kept India as a protected market. By the time the Japanese became too competitive in the 1920s, British industry couldn't compete, and Britain just closed off the empire to Japanese exports in 1932. That's a significant part of the background for World War II in the Pacific—a major part, in fact. If you looked ahead, you could see this was going to happen. But thinking ahead is not a characteristic of power centers, so-called statesmen, corporate executives. They have short-term gains that they're pursuing.

We can see it right in front of us. Look at, say, the Iraq war. It was undertaken with the expectation that it would lead to an increase in terror and nuclear proliferation, which is exactly what happened, on a scale that is far beyond what was anticipated. There is a new study just done by a couple of major terrorism specialists, Peter Bergen and others, and their estimate is that what they call "the Iraq effect"—the effect of the Iraq war on terrorism—has been a "sevenfold increase in the yearly rate of fatal jihadist attacks," focused particularly on regions and populations that have been involved in the invasion, "amounting to literally hundreds of additional terrorist attacks and thousands of civilian lives lost."[12] That's quite an increase. It's a long, careful, important study, using the Rand Corporation database.[13] I haven't seen anything about the report in the mainstream press.

You can also see this short-term thinking right now in the case of Iran. I don't know if the Bush administration is planning to invade, but in order to achieve a short-term gain in domestic political power and shifting attention away from their catastrophe in Iraq, war planners may trap themselves into invading, with consequences that are unimaginable.

Or look at North Korea. A couple of weeks ago, North Korea reached a tentative agreement about ultimately ending its nuclear programs in return for providing energy assistance.[14] The way this was described here was that North Korea had backed down and was finally agreeing to negotiations because of its isolation. What actually happened is quite different, and anyone who has been following the issue knows it, including people being quoted. In September 2005, a very far-reaching agreement was made in which North Korea committed to dismantle its nuclear weapons programs completely, and in return the United States would terminate hostile gestures and threats, would provide a light-water reactor, as had been promised years earlier, and would move toward normalization of relations with North Korea.[15] If that had been implemented, there wouldn't have been a North Korean bomb test, there wouldn't have been the current conflict, which is always verging on the edge of nuclear war.

What happened then in September 2005? A few days after the agreement, the United States forced banks to freeze North Korean assets to cut them off from the world and in effect terminated the consortium that was talking about the light-water reactor. The grounds were that North Korea was using banks for illegal transfers, for counterfeiting.[16] Well, maybe. If you look in the small print, again in today's *New York Times*, you will notice that the main bank involved, Banco Delta Asia, said it had "no evidence of such activities for North Korea."[17] The *Frankfurter Allgemeine Zeitung*, a conservative and respected German newspaper, published a report a couple of months ago that alleged that the counterfeiting was being carried out by the Central Intelligence Agency.[18] Who knows? Whatever it was, these hostile gestures toward North Korea undermined the agreement and of course drove North Korea once again to a hostile reaction, leading to a crisis. Now they're going back to something like the agreement that the United States undermined in September 2005.

It's not that these things are unpredictable. If you threaten people, they're going to create defenses.

Or take the Chinese. In a demonstration of their military capacity, the Chinese recently shot down one of their own anti-satellite systems.[19] Afterward, there was a big hubbub: China is starting the Cold War, they're a major threat, and so on. All this is totally predictable. I wrote about the possibility of this happening years ago—not because I have any insight, I was just quoting the major strategic analysts. You can read about it in *Hegemony or Survival*.[20] I quoted the Rand Corporation, leading military figures, and so on, all of whom pointed out the obvious, that other countries regard what we call "missile defense" as a first-strike weapon. A missile shield could never impede a first strike, but it could conceivably impede a retaliatory strike. So if you have a functioning missile defense system, and the adversary has no way around it, they're going to understand it as a first-strike weapon. You can attack them, and they can't retaliate.

So of course they're going to find ways around missile defense. And one of the ways to do it—and this was predicted long ago—is to destroy the U.S. satellite system, which is a lot easier than shooting down missiles. And the Chinese test is an indication that they're pursuing this approach. The same is true with the uproar about the Russian president, Vladimir Putin, re-creating the Cold War by objecting to an anti-missile system in eastern Europe.[21]

There is the speech he gave in Munich.

If you look at what he said, it is not really controversial. Maybe you don't like the tone, but the facts are correct, and there is a background to it. The Russians really have security problems. They were practically destroyed a couple of times in the last century by Germany alone. In 1990, Mikhail Gorbachev made the quite remarkable concession of allowing the unification of Germany within the NATO military alliance.[22] So a country that had practically destroyed Russia twice in that century was allowed to be part of a huge hostile military alliance, always aimed at Russia, of course. It was an incredible gesture by Gorbachev, but there was a quid pro quo. The George Bush I administration had to pledge that NATO would not expand eastward. That was the bargain. Clinton came in and broke the bargain. He expanded NATO to the east.[23] Now the United States is planning to put an anti-missile system in eastern Europe, claiming it's going to stop missiles from Iran.[24] Just think it through. Suppose Iran had nuclear weapons and missiles that could reach Europe. Under what conditions would they ever use them? In a first strike against Europe? Unless they're determined to commit suicide, Iran would never do that. Any possibility, however remote, of an Iranian missile aimed at Europe is a deterrent against U.S. attack.

The Russians have every reason to regard an anti-missile system as part of a first-strike weapon against them. Suppose the Russians were putting up an anti-missile system in Canada. Do you think the United States would cheer? We would go to war, because we understand it to be a first-strike weapon. And so do they, and so do analysts on all sides. Nevertheless we're going ahead with it, increasing the threat of destruction.

China for years has been in the lead at the United Nations in trying to establish treaties that would preserve space for peaceful uses.[25] The United States has blocked such efforts unilaterally—it goes back to Clinton, incidentally, but intensified substantially with Bush—increasing the likelihood of an arms race in space, which very significantly increases the risk of even accidental destruction. And it could mean terminal destruction. But the U.S. government proceeds, knowing the risks and just not caring about them.

Let's move on to what's happening in the media landscape. The traditional print media, newspapers and magazines, are losing readers, whereas there has been the tremendous growth of Web sites, from ZNet and Common Dreams to Counter-Punch and AlterNet. What do you see happening in terms of the media?

The media, I presume, will adjust to this with online publication with advertisements and so on. The Internet does, as you say, provide opportunities to obtain information and an extremely wide variety of viewpoints. That's a good in itself. But there is a downside. The downside is that you are so flooded with material that unless you have an understanding of the world that is sufficient to allow you to be selective, you can be drawn into completely crazed cocoons of wild interpretation. That happens all over the place. Built into the Internet is a system for creating cults. So, for example, if I had a blog, which I don't, and I put up something that is a slightly novel and maybe questionable interpretation of some event—the Bush administration is trying to poison the water in Boston or something, to pick at random—tomorrow somebody else would say, "That's right, but it's worse than you think." And pretty soon you would develop a cult of people proving that the Bush administration is trying to poison the world's water. It's extremely easy to get caught up in that kind of cultlike behavior, which has a cocoonlike property similar to other religious cults, immune to evidence, immune to argument.

So what would you suggest to someone surfing the Internet?

Surfing the Internet makes about as much sense as for, say, a biologist to read all the biology journals. You will never learn anything that way. No serious scientist does that. The literature is massive. You get flooded by it. A good scientist is one who knows what to look for, so you disregard tons of stuff and you see a little thing somewhere else. The same is true of a good newspaper reader. Whether it's in print or on the Internet, you have to know what to look for. That requires a knowledge of history, an understanding of the backgrounds, a conception of the way the media function as filters and interpreters of the world. Then you know what to look for. And the same is true on the Internet.

What do you think are going to be the archives of the future? Everything seems to be moving toward an electronic archive. How secure would they be?

Do you want them to be secure?

If you were a historian, wouldn't you?

No. If you're a historian, you want them to be open. If you look through the record of declassified documents, what you discover, I believe, is that they are very often concerned with security, but for the most part the security of the state against its own population. The state doesn't want the population to know what it's up to.

Take, say, right now. It would be nice to have the White House archives on their planning concerning Iran. They're keeping it secret, of course. Governments always keep such things secret. But are they keeping it secret from Iran or are they keeping it secret from the U.S. population, 75 percent of which already thinks we should abandon threats and turn to diplomacy?[26] I think if these archives ever come out, we'll discover they were keeping it secret from the population.

Iran knows what's happening. Washington releases information for the ears of Iranian intelligence that the planners don't even publish for the population here. Like when the Bush administration sends one hundred advanced jet bombers to Israel, advertised in the military literature as capable of bombing Iran, that's for the ears of Iranian intelligence, not the American population, so it doesn't even get published here.[27] It would be very good to see those archives right now.

So you're not too concerned about future archives being electronically stored.

Anything can be a problem, but by and large I think it's a good thing. In fact, for researchers, having the archives electronically available is a tremendous boon. I'll just talk about myself. I used to have to buy the volumes of the *Foreign Relations of the United States*, huge volumes that are in the cellar. You pore through them just to find little tidbits that are significant here and there, maybe 5 percent of the material. Now they're electronically available. You can find what you're looking for very quickly.

In recent years, there has been a marked growth in independent media, sometimes called alternative media. Amy Goodman's Democracy Now! *is on more than five hundred radio and TV stations.*

I heard of some guy in Boulder, Colorado, who is getting a lot of stuff out, too.

WHAT WE SAY GOES

I don't know about that. But there are community radio stations across the country.

It is in many places, not in all. Boston, where I live, has been singularly lacking in community radio for a long time, and still pretty much is. I travel around the country a lot, and I haven't really investigated it systematically, but my pretty strong impression is that in places that have community radio the people are more organized, active, and engaged, are working together, and so on. It's kind of a central focus from which activists can interact with each other and act cooperatively.

There is a fair amount of activism in Boston, but it's extremely atomized. One group doesn't know what another group is doing a couple miles away. If there were something more central, that problem could be overcome. And community radio performs that service, apart from providing the kinds of materials that you get on *Democracy Now!* or on your programs at *Alternative Radio.*

It's almost become a cliché that as long as there is no draft or economic collapse, people are too complacent and too comfortable to fight power. Do you accept that?

I think the evidence for that view is very slim. The talk about the draft was an excuse by Vietnam War supporters to try to explain why the population had turned so strongly against the war at a time when elites had not yet really turned against it. They said, "It's because people are afraid they're going to get drafted." There is very limited evidence to support that. In fact, by 1969, around 70 percent of the general population described the war as "fundamentally wrong and immoral," not as a "mistake."[28] They didn't say, "We don't like it because our children are getting drafted." I think those are largely fabrications by apologists for state violence.

What about economic collapse?

The same thing. Was there an economic collapse in the 1960s, when major social programs were instituted as a result of popular pressure—the civil rights movement, Medicare, social benefits, and so on? It was not the result of economic collapse. That was a period of peak economic progress. Or take, say, the 1980s. For most of the population the period since the 1970s has been pretty gloomy. Real incomes have stagnated or declined. Nevertheless, there was no economic collapse in the 1980s. But it was a period of tremendous activism. For example, the Latin American solidarity movements—something new after hundreds of years of Western imperialism—developed in the 1980s. The feminist movement didn't develop as a result of economic collapse. The global justice movements of the 1990s, which are extremely important, developed during a brief period of economic boom. I just don't think the correlations work.

In the 1980s, you and Edward Herman wrote Manufacturing Consent.[29] *Of course, then the Soviet Union was the archenemy of the United States. If you were revising the book today, might you insert Al Qaeda in there as the organizing principle for U.S. hegemony?*

Actually, we did revise the book. We published a second edition in 2002. We didn't change the text, but we wrote a new introduction that does contain a note of self-criticism on several issues.[30] For example, we used the term *anticommunism* to describe one of five filters we had listed as factors in shaping perspective.[31] And that was just too narrow. Is it Al Qaeda now? It's the threat of vague "Islamic terrorism," which, incidentally, we're inciting. We're inciting jihadi terrorism, and then calling it a pretext for carrying out aggressive wars.

There are very interesting studies of jihadi terrorism. The most important scholarly studies I know of are by Fawaz Gerges, who is originally Lebanese and teaches at Sarah Lawrence College. He's done extensive studies of the jihadi movements—the most reliable and extensive that are available, as far as I know—conducting interviews, studying their literature, and so on.[32] He made some interesting discoveries. For example, he discovered that after 9/11 the jihadi leadership, the clerics and others, bitterly condemned Osama bin Laden and wanted to disassociate themselves from him. The attacks were totally the wrong thing to do and un-Islamic. Everything was wrong with them in principle and tactics. But the Bush administration managed to reforge unity among various jihadists through its own aggressiveness, militancy, and violence. That brought them back together. An alternative option, which, of course, Gerges recommends, is that the United States should have used that opportunity to isolate the extreme Islamic militants, the Osama bin Laden types, even from the jihadis. That would have made a much more peaceful world.

So you make a distinction between bin Laden, Al Qaeda, and jihadis in general.

For one thing, it is now recognized that what's considered the Islamic Al Qaeda is what some call a "network of networks," a loosely associated network of groups more or less acting on their own, maybe inspired by bin Laden as a kind of mythic leader, and having similar goals.[33] On the other hand, that network of networks has been solidified by Bush administration actions. That's why, for example, Michael Scheuer, who for many years was the top CIA official tracking Osama bin Laden, describes Bush as bin Laden's "only indispensable ally."[34] That's not an unusual description. And it's supported by the facts.

What do you think of Samuel Huntington's "clash of civilizations" idea? He wrote, "Islam's borders are bloody, and so are its innards."[35]

As history, it's ridiculous. Christianity has been far more violent for centuries—in fact, one of the most savage civilizations in history. As a description of what was happening at the time Huntington wrote, it was just overwhelmingly refuted by the facts, overwhelmingly. At the time he wrote, the most valued and oldest U.S. ally in the Middle East was Saudi Arabia—as it still is today—because it had all the oil. It's the most extreme fundamentalist state in the world. The United States has been supporting extreme Islamic fundamentalism as a weapon against secular nationalism for years. So the most extreme fundamentalist tyranny in the world is our major ally.

The most populous Islamic country is Indonesia. Up until 1965, the United States was pretty hostile to Indonesia because it was moving on a path of independence. But when the Suharto coup took place, with U.S. backing, and slaughtered hundreds of thousands, peasants mostly, destroyed the only mass political organization, and opened the place to Western exploitation, it became a great friend. And Suharto remained "our kind of guy," as the Clinton administration described him, right to the end of his bloody rule, one of the most vicious in the world.[36] The U.S. ambassador under Reagan, Paul Wolfowitz, the great exponent of democracy, was bitterly condemned by human rights activists and democracy activists in Indonesia for undermining them at every point. So, the biggest Islamic country in the world was our wonderful ally as long as it was playing its role in the U.S. world system.

Or take the Catholic Church. As we discussed earlier, the U.S. wars in Central America in the 1980s were to a large extent wars against the Catholic Church. So where is the clash of civilizations?

There is some truth, though, to what Huntington predicted. There are people who are desperately trying to create a clash of civilizations. Two of the leading ones are Osama bin Laden and George Bush. So it could happen.

There is a quote from Orwell in 1984. He says, "It was not desirable that the proles should have strong political feelings. All that was required of them was a primitive patriotism which could be appealed to whenever it was necessary to make them accept longer working hours or shorter rations. And even when they became discontented, as they sometimes did, their discontent led nowhere, because without general ideas, they could only focus it on petty specific grievances. The larger evils invariably escaped their notice."[37]

Orwell was talking about a brutal, vicious, totalitarian state. We don't live in that kind of society. Efforts will be made to create such systems, but to resist them and overcome them is vastly easier than in the kind of society he was describing. This is a very free society, after all. The state has very little power to coerce.

EIGHT

WHAT WE CAN DO

The title of this book is What We Say Goes. *Can you tell me when that was said, and provide some examples?*

The statement was made by George Bush I in February 1991.[1] It was toward the end of the first Gulf War, when he said proudly that there is a "new world order" that we're establishing and the main principle of this new world order is "what we say goes."[2]

Some examples? Take one that didn't work out quite as expected, the second invasion of Iraq, this invasion. Bush II, Colin Powell, and others made it very clear to the United Nations that either they could go along with the U.S. plans to invade Iraq or they would be, as it was put, "irrelevant."[3] It was put even more brazenly by the UN ambassador John

Bolton: "There is no United Nations."[4] If we choose to have the UN's acquiescence, then it can go along with us. Otherwise not. And, of course, the invasion of Iraq was undertaken against overwhelming international opposition. There were international polls taken. Outside of Israel and maybe India, there was practically undetectable support. I don't think it went over 10 percent anywhere in Europe.[5] But what we say goes. If we want to do it, we do it.

With Bush II, the stance happens to be extreme, but it's not an unusual position. It's understandable on the part of a superpower that has overwhelming military force, incomparable security, a huge economic base, and no real rivals in the world. The United States had the same attitude right through the Cold War as well, though not in as extreme a form because there was always the threat of Soviet or Chinese deterrence.

A very clear example of that, which people keep bringing up today, with a mistaken interpretation, is Vietnam. The major part of the U.S. war by far was waged against South Vietnam. North Vietnam was kind of a sideshow. But the protest and concern about the war, including most of the peace movement, was almost entirely about North Vietnam. If you look back at Pentagon planning, which we now know in detail from the Pentagon Papers and later releases, the bombing of the North was planned in meticulous detail: where you bomb, and where you don't, and when. There is practically nothing about the bombing of the South, which was at maybe triple the scale of the North by 1965. If you look at Robert McNamara's memoirs, he discusses in detail the plans for the bombing of the North. He doesn't even mention some of the major decisions of the war—like the decision in late January 1965 to use jet bombers to escalate the bombing of South Vietnam.[6]

Why? Because in the South what we say goes. There was no cost to us and no international opposition, so we could do what we wanted. In the North, in contrast, it was hazardous. There were foreign embassies in Hanoi and Russian ships in Haiphong harbor. They were bombing a Chinese railroad that happened to pass through North Vietnam, and it was visible on the world stage. And also, the North had defenses. They had Soviet anti-aircraft, which was described as "interference" in the affairs of Vietnam. We couldn't bomb as freely as we liked. So there it wasn't quite true that what we say goes. But in the South it was.

The same with Cambodia or Laos. They were completely defenseless. Nobody cared except peace movement people, so you could bomb at will. Nobody cares now, either. So what we say goes as long as there is no threat, no danger. As long as it's costless to us, what we say goes. By the early 1990s, when Bush made the statement, it looked as if there wasn't going to be much cost to anything. The United States had just invaded Panama, killed maybe a couple thousand people, mostly poor people in the slums, vetoed a couple of UN Security Council resolutions, and so on.[7] But nobody was going to do anything about it. So what we say goes.

Over the years, you've commented on the correlation between human rights violations and what's called U.S. aid. Is that pattern continuing?

To give credit where credit is due, this is Ed Herman's work, which was incorporated in our joint book *The Political Economy of Human Rights* and is spelled out in detail elsewhere in his own writings.[8] He's an economist, as you know, and he did a careful study of relations between U.S. aid and torture and found a quite dramatic correlation.

This correlation has also been noticed by others. One of the leading, maybe the leading academic specialist on human rights in Latin America, Lars Schoultz at North Carolina, published an article back in 1981 pointing out that U.S. "aid has tended to flow disproportionately to Latin American governments which torture their citizens" and "to the hemisphere's relatively egregious violators of fundamental human rights."[9] That included military aid, and went on right through the Carter administration. I don't think anybody has bothered to check it for the Reagan years because it was so transparently obvious. And it continues right up until today. Right through the Clinton years, Colombia was by far the leading recipient of U.S. aid, and also had by far the worst human rights record in Latin America.[10] That alone makes the point.

In fact, if you look at the leading recipients of U.S. aid, most of it military aid, two countries are in a separate category: Israel and Egypt, which gets half the aid given to Israel. This arrangement is part of the Camp David agreements from back in 1979, unofficially. Aid to Egypt is basically aid to Israel, to encourage Egypt to sort of play along. But aid to Israel and Egypt is in a separate category, way above anybody else. If you look at the rest, the leading recipients of U.S. aid have typically been among the worst human rights offenders.

Pakistan, for example, or Turkey.

In the late 1980s it was El Salvador. Then it switched to Turkey during the years of the Clinton-backed massive atrocities in Turkey against the Kurds in the 1990s. And then by, I think, about 1999, Turkey was replaced by Colombia. The reason, which was transparent, was that Turkey had succeeded in crushing any resistance to its atrocities, so it didn't need the military aid that much. And Colombia was still engaged in vicious and violent counterinsurgency campaigns.

It's usually called a "drug war" in the U.S. press. It has very little to do with reducing drug use in the United States and is known to have no effect on it. It's basically chemical warfare carried out against *campesinos*, Afro-Colombians, indigenous people, destroying their crops, driving them off the land and into the urban slums, leading to a lot of deaths. Colombia has one of the largest displaced-persons populations in the world.[11] The government effectively clears land for mining, hydroelectric plants, export-oriented agribusiness, ranching, mineral extraction. It's also destroying the biodiversity of one of the richest areas of the world.

You were there.

I took hours of testimonies from poor peasants whose lives had been destroyed, whose lands had been destroyed, whose children were dying, and who were being driven away. It's chemical warfare. It also happens to destroy coca, but the government's own studies show that if there were really any interest in cutting back drug use in the United States, by far the most cost-effective means is prevention and treatment.[12] Police measures are far more expensive and less effective. Still more ineffective and costly is border interdiction. And by far the least effective and most costly is out-of-country operations, like eradicating crops, which means chemical warfare.

But they do it, because reducing the use of drugs is not the goal. Some of the figures are striking. The British journalists Sue Branford and Hugh O'Shaughnessy point out in a recent book on Colombia that the aid the European Union gives for alternative crops for farmers who are producing coca or poppies is lower than their subsidies to the tobacco industries.[13] Tobacco is a far greater killer than hard drugs. But for Europe, subsidizing your own tobacco industry, a huge killer, takes more money than finding alternative crops for poor peasants who are relying on opium or poppy cultivation to survive.

You've said it was significant when Wall Street turned against the Vietnam War. That was around 1968.

Yes, 1968. It was after the Tet Offensive, which convinced the business world that the war was just not worth it. They understood pretty well that the United States had basically won the war, and continuing it was just too costly.

Why hasn't the business community turned on the war in Iraq?

There is no comparison between the two cases. That's all doctrinal fanaticism. The only comparison between Vietnam and Iraq is the way it's described in the United States. In both cases the framework is that it's costing us a lot, it's a "quagmire."

The business community is only going to turn against this war if it really becomes extremely costly to the United

States and to their own interests. But that will take a lot. It's not at all comparable to Vietnam, which was much less important strategically from their point of view.

There have been many reports about potential U.S. military action against Iran.

The nature of the discussion about attacking Iran is what might it cost us. It's kind of intriguing that few see what they're saying. Just as Bush announced the "surge" in Iraq, in sharp opposition to public opinion in the United States—and in Iraq, but who cares about that—they started leaking information about alleged Iranian supplies to the insurgents, who were killing U.S. soldiers.[14]

Then a debate rages, a technical debate. Do the serial numbers on the improvised explosive devices really trace back to Iran? Does the leadership of Iran know or only the Revolutionary Guards? And we have kind of sophisticated discussions about that. It's a textbook illustration of how sophisticated propaganda works. Sophisticated propaganda does not hammer home the party line. That's what they do in totalitarian states, where nobody even believes the propaganda because the source is too flagrantly obvious. The proper way for a propaganda system to work is to insinuate the party line as a presupposition—so you don't even discuss it, you just accept it—and then to allow, in fact encourage, vigorous debate on the basis of that presupposition. That's just what's happening.

The presupposition is that the United States owns the world. If that's not the case, if you reject that, then you can't debate whether Iran is interfering in Iraq. It's kind of like debating whether the Allies were interfering in Vichy France in 1943, when it was under German rule. Only if you accept the assumption that the United States rules the world by right can you then ask whether someone else is interfering in a country that we invaded and occupied. That's the way the debate goes on. That's the core of the party line. One corollary is that the only thing that matters is the costs to us.

Do you trace the roots of this idea to the "Grand Area" strategy, the planning documents that were formulated in the early 1940s by the Council on Foreign Relations?[15]

And the State Department.

Is that still operative?

The documents are interesting because they articulate with some clarity the general thinking in elite circles. During the Second World War, there were high-level meetings of State Department officials and the Council on Foreign Relations, which is the major extragovernmental source of foreign policy discussion and advice, and they laid out a picture of the postwar world, which was then pursued with some degree of faithfulness in the years that followed, not surprisingly.

The same principles are now operative. It was assumed during the Second World War—to be precise, in the early years, 1939 to 1943—that the war would end with two major powers: Germany and the United States. Germany would be dominant in parts of Eurasia, and the United States would take over the Middle East, the Western hemisphere, and the former British Empire. That was supposed to be the Grand Area.

As the war went on, by 1943 to 1944, it was obvious Germany was going to be defeated, and the Grand Area was then expanded to as much of the world as the United States could dominate. The goal was to create a liberal international order in which U.S.-based corporations would be free to operate. Remember, the United States was so much in advance of anyone else after wartime destruction. In fact, the United States gained from the war: industrial production tripled or quadrupled while most U.S. rivals were devastated or at least weakened. The United States emerged with about half the world's wealth, so a liberal international order was tolerable. You could have relatively free competition with assurance that the playing field was tilted in the right direction, to use the common metaphor. It would be an international system in which U.S. corporations would be free to access resources, access markets, invest without constraints. That's the basic conception of the international order.

You've said that the Grand Area strategy essentially extended the Monroe Doctrine, which was limited to this hemisphere, to the rest of the world.

The Monroe Doctrine, remember, was a hope for the future. The United States did not have the power in the 1820s to implement the Monroe Doctrine. They couldn't even conquer Cuba, which was one of the main goals in the 1820s of John Quincy Adams and others. Also, they couldn't conquer Canada. The United States repeatedly invaded Canada and was beaten back. At the time, John Quincy Adams pointed out that we couldn't conquer Cuba because of the British naval deterrent, but sooner or later Cuba would fall into our hands by the laws of "political gravitation," much as an apple falls from the tree.[16] Meaning, over time we would become more powerful, and Britain relatively weaker, so we would eventually be able to conquer Cuba—which in fact happened. In 1898, the United States invaded Cuba under the guise of liberating it but in fact to prevent its liberation from Spain and to turn it into a virtual colony until 1959.

In all the discussions about the U.S. military prison in Guantánamo Bay, there is no mention of how Guantánamo came under U.S. control.

Guantánamo was essentially taken at the point of a gun by the United States under what was called a treaty, but Cuba at the time was occupied by the United States. It was sign the treaty or else. So Cuba granted the United States rights for a coaling station at the base in Guantánamo. Coaling stations were important in those days. But that was it, essentially. Years later, Cuba tried to get out of the treaty, but the United States wouldn't allow it. So Fidel Castro has been refusing to accept the small payment for Guantánamo the United States makes every year.[17]

The United States is completely violating the illegitimate treaty that it imposed. It's not using it as a coaling station. The United States also violated the treaty before when it started using Guantánamo for Haitian refugees. Washington wouldn't live up to the requirement under the Universal Declaration of Human Rights that "everyone has the right to seek and to enjoy in other countries asylum from persecution."[18] So it shipped the refugees off to what amounted to a prison in Guantánamo.[19] And now the United States is using Guantánamo for prisoners Washington wants to be able to hold outside any domestic or international law. The Supreme Court has argued that it can't rule on the rights of Guantánamo detainees because Guantánamo is not under U.S. jurisdiction, and the Bush administration and Congress effectively say Guantánamo is not under international law.[20] So it's a convenient torture chamber.

There's no need to debate, really, what goes on in Guantánamo. First of all, it's totally illegal even to send people there. If they weren't intending to use Guantánamo as a torture chamber, why not bring people to a prison in New York? As soon as you see that they're sending them to Guantánamo, you know it's for activities in violation of international human rights law. You don't have to investigate any further.

There are by now other reasons for the United States to maintain Guantánamo, which would be Cuba's major port. Holding on to Guantánamo prevents Cuba from using it as a port and prevents development of the eastern end of the island. So it's part of the strangulation of Cuba, the punishment of Cubans for what the Democratic administrations of the early 1960s called its "successful defiance" of U.S. policies going back to the Monroe Doctrine.[21]

Very much like defiance against the Mafia don: it can't be tolerated.

It can't be tolerated. In fact, international affairs has more than a slight resemblance to the Mafia.

You often make that analogy in your talks.

I think it's real. By and large, the state acts as something like the executive agency of those who largely own the domestic society in the United States, the corporate sector. It's a pretty standard feature of state policy. But there are some striking cases where state policy runs counter even to corporate goals. You see some interesting examples of conflict between state and corporate interests. It's kind of an interesting topic for the study of international affairs. Cuba is one example. U.S. agribusiness, even U.S. energy corporations, would be quite eager to overcome the strangling embargo on Cuba, which they see as a market and as an investment opportunity. Agribusiness would love to have Cuba as a market. The U.S. pharmaceutical industry is interested in Cuba's quite advanced biotechnology industry. But, most strikingly, energy corporations are interested in exploiting Cuban offshore oil in the Gulf of Mexico, which is apparently estimated to be substantial. But the state will not permit it.[22] Of course, the majority of the U.S. population, which doesn't count, is in favor of establishing diplomatic relations with Cuba.[23] But that's irrelevant. What's interesting is business interests are blocked, in pretty striking ways.

You may recall that about a year ago there was a meeting in Mexico City between the Cuban energy specialists and representatives of Texas oil companies and also some of the majors, like ExxonMobil. The Bush administration comes straight out of that sector. But the Bush administration discovered that the meeting was being held in a Sheraton hotel, which is owned by a U.S.

corporation, so they ordered the hotel to break up the meeting and expel the Texas oil representatives and the Cubans.[24] It was a slap in the face to George Bush's friends and supporters. But state interests, the Mafia-style interests, overwhelmed even the interests of the core constituency of the Bush administration.

The same is happening in Iran. U.S. oil companies would be delighted to help enter into the development of huge Iranian natural gas and oil fields, but they're blocked by the state.[25] We have to punish Iran for its successful defiance in overthrowing a U.S.-imposed tyrant.

This morning, the *Boston Globe* reported something that has been known around here for a long time. In 1974, presumably at U.S. government initiative, MIT made a deal with the shah of Iran to effectively lease the nuclear engineering department, or a large part of it, to Iran, to bring in lots of Iranian nuclear engineers and train them in the development of uranium enrichment and other techniques of nuclear development. In return, the shah, who was one of the most brutal tyrants of the period, with a horrible human rights record, would pay MIT at least half a million dollars. The article also points out that several of the engineers who were trained at MIT are now apparently running the Iranian nuclear programs.[26] Those programs were strongly supported by the United States in the mid-1970s.

By Henry Kissinger and Gerald Ford.

Yes, and by Rumsfeld, Cheney, Wolfowitz, and others. They claimed at the time that Iran needed nuclear power. It didn't have enough energy, and needed to preserve its hydrocarbon resources for other purposes. Now the same people are giving the opposite story. They say how can Iran possibly be developing nuclear power? They have so much oil. They must be developing weapons.[27] These are the same people.

In the 1970s, there was quite a conflict at MIT about this program. I was there. When the news leaked out, the students were pretty upset, and there was a lot of protest. It led to a student referendum, which opposed the deal, by maybe 80 percent or something. By then, it had caused enough of an uproar that there had to be a faculty meeting. Everybody showed up and there was lively debate. Only a very small number of people—I was one of them—opposed the arrangement. The faculty overwhelmingly voted for it. It was implemented and continued until the fall of the shah.

Inside of Iran there are actually shortages of gasoline and consumer-grade petrochemical products.

That's correct, partly because of Iran's domestic policies, but partly it's just that Iran took a tremendous battering. The 1980s war with Iraq, backed by the United States and Britain and other European powers, including Russia, killed hundreds of thousands of Iranians and shattered a lot of the country. It's quite something to overcome.

And much of the battlefield was in the oil-rich areas of Khuzestan.

Precisely.

They're talking now in Iran of introducing rationing.

Yes. In fact, they are importing oil.[28]

Hrant Dink, a Turkish-Armenian journalist and editor, was assassinated in Istanbul on January 19. He had been charged with something called "insulting Turkish identity" because he talked about the genocide of the Armenians more than nine decades ago.[29] Orhan Pamuk, the Nobel Prize winner, has fled Turkey under death threats, and another novelist, Elif Shafak, rarely leaves her home because of threats against her.[30] Why is it so difficult for Turkey to acknowledge what happened in the 1915 period? The documentation is staggering.

Not only that. A publisher who translated some books of mine was just on trial this year—he had been a couple years earlier—because there was a brief discussion of the huge atrocities against the Kurds in the 1990s.[31] That's also punishable. The case was dropped, but others still continue.

Countries do not concede their atrocities. There is, obviously, plenty of condemnation for the German atrocities. We're happy to talk about them. But how many memorials do you know of in the United States for the Native American population or for slaves? That's not ancient history, it's very much alive. Why is the incarceration rate for blacks far higher than for whites? Where are the remnants of indigenous Americans? Until the 1960s, the history was barely even acknowledged. In fact, there were immense lies about it, even in scholarship. Now, thanks to the 1960s activism, it's at least acknowledged, but barely.

Israel, which is an ally of Turkey, is also reluctant to use the term genocide *about the Armenians. In fact, several years ago, Shimon Peres said that there was no genocide.*[32]

That's true. Back, I think, around the early 1980s, there was a genocide conference in Israel run by a scholar who specializes on the topic, Israel Charny. Elie Wiesel was supposed to chair it. The government of Menachem Begin effectively ordered them to eliminate the Armenian genocide from the conference since Turkey is their very close ally. Wiesel withdrew as chair. Charny went ahead and included the topic, but over the government's strong objections.[33]

What is the military and economic relationship between Israel and Turkey?

We don't know the details because it's kept secret, but it started formally in 1958 with a 'military alliance. According to Israeli specialists on this, it's a very close military and economic relationship.[34] They describe it as Israel's second most important international alliance after the United States. Much of it is kept under wraps, but it's pretty clear that the Israeli air force is using the U.S. bases in eastern Turkey at least for reconnaissance.[35] Maybe they have nuclear-armed bombers there. You can only speculate.

What does Turkey get out of it?

Turkey is a part of the whole U.S.-organized Middle East system. Turkey is a major military and economic ally. It's a powerful state right on the borders of the oil-rich Middle East. Israel is another component of the alliance. Israel alone, as an offshoot of the United States, has air and armored forces that are larger and technologically more advanced than those of any NATO power outside of the United States, including Turkey. So Israel and Turkey have high-tech military relations, as well as a common interest as part of the peripheral system by which the United States tries to control the Middle East. They have common interests in other areas, too. Turkey happens to be water-rich and Israel is water-poor, for example. Israel can provide technological assistance to Turkey. It's a natural relationship.

The United States has just established a new military command for Africa.[36] *The United States has a military base in Djibouti. There is a new war front in the continent's northeast quadrant. What are U.S. goals there?*

The French military had a base in Djibouti, which the United States has taken over.[37] Somalia, its neighbor, is right across from the Arabian peninsula, where the world's main energy resources are. Ethiopia, which also borders Djibouti, is a strong U.S. ally right now. Ethiopia—which like Israel has never declared its final borders and has intentions, apparently, of extending its borders over Somalia and Eritrea—invaded Somalia to eliminate what appeared to be a fairly stable Islamist government, with U.S. backing and in strict violation of a Security Council resolution.[38] In December 2006, the United States initiated and pushed through Security Council Resolution 1725, which recognized the government in Somalia that was holding on to a tiny corner of the country.[39] The resolution also explicitly demanded that neighboring states not interfere in Somalia's internal affairs.[40] Instantly the Ethiopian invasion followed, in violation of the U.S.-initiated resolution strongly supported here, and instituted an Ethiopian-run government with U.S. support.[41]

The Bush administration hopes Somalia will be another U.S. ally, along with Ethiopia. This alliance—Ethiopia, Djibouti, Somalia—gives the United States a powerful base right in the Horn of Africa, which is right next door to the major energy-producing regions. In addition to that, there is West Africa, which is quite a substantial source of energy, oil in particular. And Africa has plenty of resources to exploit, in the Congo, for example. So the renewed interest in Africa is not too surprising. I think the main goal is a firmer grip on Middle East energy resources.

Colin Powell was fairly quick to describe the killings in Darfur, a region of Sudan, as "genocide."[42]

Colin Powell is one of the people who dragged his feet slightly in calling it genocide. But Darfur is a big issue in the United States and the West now, and a very convenient one. It's convenient because there are major atrocities undoubtedly being carried out by an official enemy. You can attribute the atrocities to Arabs, so it's perfect. Just the kind of atrocities we love. Of course, there are no serious proposals to do anything about them. The proposals are all in the form of "Why don't *you* do something about it?"

It's also a complicated issue, not simply an issue of evil Arabs, a terrible tyrant carrying out genocide, the sort of standard story here, which has some element of truth to it but is by no means the whole story. There is a longtime conflict between nomadic groups and settled peasants that is becoming much worse, probably as one of the consequences of global warming, because the territories for grazing and agriculture have been adversely affected. In the Sudan, the United States did play a constructive role in bringing about at least a tentative peaceful settlement in the civil war between south and north. But major atrocities are carried out on all sides, and among the peasant-based tribes.

There is a very good article about Darfur in the *London Review of Books* by Mahmood Mamdani, who has the disadvantage of actually knowing something about Darfur—so, unfortunately, he tells a complicated story.[43] He's particularly critical of the kind of line that's taken by people like the *New York Times* columnist Nicholas Kristof, who vastly oversimplify what's going on in Darfur and strike moral postures about it. There are atrocities, serious ones, and surely something should be done about them. Regrettably, they're by no means the worst in the region, not even close. The worst in the region are in eastern Congo, where millions of people have been killed in the last few years, as Mamdani points out. Nobody is talking about that because it doesn't conveniently fit into an appropriate ideological framework. Besides, you might be able to do something about it.

I was interested that you said that Israel and Ethiopia have no recognized, defined borders. You talked about Ethiopia, but what about Israel?

Israel has never established its borders. In fact, it's very systematically expanding its borders, with U.S. support.

Everything that Israel does, virtually, is with the authorization of the United States and with its diplomatic, economic, military, and ideological support. It's been expanding illegally into the occupied territories. The wall Israel is building cuts through the West Bank, surrounds Jewish settlements, takes much of the arable land and the most valuable resource, water, and renders a lot of Palestinian territories virtually unviable. The fragments that are left to Palestinians are broken up with hundreds of checkpoints and other barriers to prevent easy transportation and so on.[44]

The phrase "right to exist" is used constantly. When did that become part of the conversation?

I've never seen a detailed study of it, but my strong impression is that the concept of Israel's right to exist was either invented or at least reached prominence in the mid-1970s, probably as a reaction to the fact that the major Arab states, with the backing of the PLO, had accepted Israel's right to exist within recognized and secure borders.[45]

That means the 1949 UN boundaries?

Yes, the recognized international border. The Arabs recognized the right of every state in the region to exist, including Israel, within secure and recognized borders. That included, by 1976, a Palestinian state in the occupied territories. Actually, this came to the United Nations in January 1976 in a resolution advanced by the major Arab states, the so-called confrontation states of Syria, Jordan, and Egypt, with the backing of the PLO and others. The United States vetoed the resolution, so it's out of history.[46] But the United States realized at the time, I presume, that they were going to have to set the barriers higher if they wanted to prevent a diplomatic settlement. It wouldn't do just to keep to the right to exist within secure and recognized borders. You have to prevent diplomacy. That's when the concept "right to exist" began to appear prominently. To demand that the Palestinians, or Arabs, or for that matter anyone, accept Israel's right to exist is to grant Israel something that no state in the international system has. No state is granted a right to exist. They're recognized, but not granted a right to exist.

In the case of Israel, that would require the Palestinians to recognize the legitimacy of their expulsion—not just the fact but its legitimacy. It's as if Mexico were required to accept the right of the United States to exist on half of Mexico, gained by conquest. Mexicans don't accept that, nor should they. Almost every border in the world is the result of conquest. The borders are recognized, but nobody goes on to demand that the legitimacy be recognized, especially by a population that was driven out.

More than five decades ago, you and your wife considered living in Israel, but it didn't pan out. Why not?

For complicated personal reasons. We came pretty close. We were both eager to do it. We wanted to live in a kibbutz. But life takes complicated turns. There was no ideological reason that blocked it. I probably wouldn't have lasted very long.

But I recall your telling me that you had encountered in Israel quite racist attitudes toward Arabs, which disturbed you.

That was unmistakable, absolutely unmistakable. Not only toward Arabs but toward Moroccan Jews—the Sephardim—which was in a way even more extreme than the racism toward Arabs.

One assumption people make about you is that there is some urgent connection between your work in linguistics and your political activism.

It's a very strange assumption. As far as my political work is concerned, I might as well be an algebraic topologist. There are some remote, abstract connections having to do with foundations of human nature, mostly speculative at this point. I've written about these questions, some of which go back to discussions during the Enlightenment. But it has no practical consequences for human affairs.

In your book Perilous Power, *which you wrote with Gilbert Achcar, you say, "Educating the American public is the main thing to be done."[47] You write books, give lectures, and do interviews like this. That's your effort in terms of education. What about a broader initiative in terms of educating the U.S. public? Do you have any suggestions?*

Just the obvious one. Individuals can't do it. It doesn't make any sense. People have to do it locally. That's exactly the importance of labor unions. They did defend workers' rights, but beyond that they were very influential in workers' education. I remember this from childhood, when my family—seamstresses, shop boys, unemployed working-class Jewish immigrants—were members of labor unions. That's where there were workers' education centers, cultural centers, cultural events, newspapers. In the early part of the twentieth century, there were all sorts of labor newspapers that reached hundreds of thousands of people.[48] That was a source of popular education. Unions have been under bitter business and government attack, partly for that reason. But it's possible to reconstruct popular education in all kinds of ways, in fact to influence even the schools. But it's going to have to be done by lots of people, just as in every other case.

Where did the civil rights movement come from? It didn't happen because Martin Luther King said, "Let's have a civil rights movement." He was riding the wave of popular activism. And the same with Lyndon Johnson's progressive measures, which were not insignificant. He played a role in them, but a wave of popular activism demanded them. It's the same with anything else. Did Betty Friedan say, "Let's have women's rights," and all of a sudden we had women's rights? No. It's a long struggle. That's what education is.

In Failed States, *you point out that often critics of the system are denounced for being negative and never having anything positive to put forth. You address that criticism with some specific suggestions about solutions.*[49]

Very unoriginal suggestions that just happen to be supported by a large majority of people in the United States. I think they're good suggestions. They would change the country significantly. There is nothing radical about them, but they're off the agenda. That's part of the serious collapse of democratic institutions.

Let me just read some of your suggestions in Failed States: *accept the jurisdiction of the International Criminal Court and the World Court, sign and carry forward the Kyoto Protocols, let the United Nations take the lead in international crises, rely on diplomatic and economic measures rather than military ones in confronting terror, keep to the traditional interpretation of the UN Charter, give up the Security Council veto.*

Let me add, that means no use of force except in self-defense.

That would be under Article 51.

Yes. But real self-defense against an ongoing or perhaps imminent armed attack.

And the others: cut back sharply on military spending and sharply increase social spending. I remember years ago you told me that the United States should be an organizers' paradise. Do you still feel that way?

I still think it's an organizers' paradise, and a lot of good things are happening. You see them all over. I gave a talk a few days ago in downtown Boston at the annual meeting of a wonderful group called Vida Urbana. They were beginning their thirty-fourth year of organizing and activism in the poorest areas of Boston, mostly Latino and black. A terrific group of people. There were a lot of people there who were very enthusiastic. It was a lively meeting. It was also the opening of a three-day conference of radical organizers from around the country who were doing similar work. So things are happening, and a lot of them. The numbers of people involved are very high, probably higher than the 1960s, I'm convinced, but they are atomized, scattered. The one real success of power systems in the United States has been to separate people from one another, so you don't know what's happening. I knew very little about this group, though it's been here for thirty-four years and has been very effective right in my own city.

Eqbal Ahmad gave a talk at MIT on the role of intellectuals in October 1998, just about six months before he died in Islamabad. He said, "You have to be willing to take risks." He was talking about intellectuals. The other thing that Ahmad said was that "love of people is central."[50]

Eqbal was a very close old friend, but I don't entirely agree with him on that. First of all, we don't face serious risks here in taking dissident positions or even engaging in resistance activities. Yes, there are risks, but compared with what most people face in the world, they're undetectable. You get denounced by whoever it is, you're ridiculed, you're vilified. Maybe you can't get invited to the right dinner parties. But are those risks? Think what most people really face. People are called intellectuals because they're privileged. It's not because they're smart or they know a lot. There are plenty of people who know more and are smarter but aren't intellectuals because they don't have the privilege. The people called intellectuals are privileged. They have resources and opportunities, and enough freedom has been won so that the state does not have an unrestrained capacity to repress. It has some but not much—nowhere near what people claim. There are cases here where intolerable things happen—people get thrown out of their jobs—but, by and large, the risks that privileged people face here are very small. So I don't even think it's a question of taking risks. It's a matter of being decent.

Love of people? Yes, of course, or at least commitment to them and their needs.

NOTES

1. WHAT WE SAY GOES

1. James Traub, "Why Not Build a Bomb?" *New York Times Magazine*, 29 January 2006.
2. Saint Augustine, *The City of God* (1467), part 1, book 4, chap. 4. See also Noam Chomsky, *Pirates and Emperors, Old and New: International Terrorism in the Real World* (Cambridge, Mass.: South End Press, 2002), p. vii.
3. Editorial, "Straight Talk Needed on Pakistan," *New York Times*, 28 January 2006.
4. *Judgment of the International Military Tribunal for the Trial of German Major War Criminals*, Nuremberg, Germany, 30 September and 1 October 1946.
5. Howard Friel and Richard Falk, *The Record of the Paper: How the New York Times Misreports U.S. Foreign Policy* (New York: Verso, 2004). See also Friel and Falk, *Israel–Palestine on the Record: How the New York Times Misreports Conflict in the Middle East* (New York: Verso, 2007).
6. Falk and Friel, *Record of the Paper*, p. 15.
7. Martin Luther King Jr., "Beyond Vietnam," in *Voices of a People's History of the United States*, ed. Howard Zinn and Anthony Arnove (New York: Seven Stories Press, 2004), p. 423.
8. Howard Zinn, "The Problem Is Civil Obedience," in ibid., pp. 483–84.

9. See, for example, editorial, "Dr. King's Error," *New York Times,* 7 April 1967, written three days after King's "Beyond Vietnam" speech.

2. LEBANON AND THE CRISIS IN THE MIDDLE EAST

1. Greg Myre and Steven Erlanger, "Clashes Spread to Lebanon as Hezbollah Raids Israel," *New York Times,* 13 July 2006.
2. Alec Russell, "Bush Lays the Blame on Hizbollah Aggression," *Daily Telegraph* (London), 14 July 2006.
3. See, among other reports, Human Rights Watch, "Release All Fifteen Lebanese Hostages," 18 April 2000, online at http://hrw .org/english/docs/2000/04/18/isrlpa486.htm.
4. Kerem Shalom, "2 Israeli Troops Killed in Attack," *Los Angeles Times,* 26 June 2006.
5. United Nations, "Statement on Gaza by United Nations Humanitarian Agencies Working in the Occupied Palestinian Territory," media release, 3 August 2006; United Nations Office for the Coordination of Humanitarian Affairs, *Humanitarian Monitor: Occupied Palestinian Territory,* no. 2 (June 2006).
6. On June 24, 2006, Osama and Mustafa Abu Muamar were abducted by the Israel Defense Forces in Al Shouka, near Rafah. Josh Brannon, "IDF Commandos Enter Gaza, Capture Two Hamas Terrorists," *Jerusalem Post,* 25 June 2006; Lesley White, "The Kidnap of This Woman's Husband Sparked the Latest War in the Middle East," *Sunday Times Magazine* (London), 19 November 2006.
7. Agence France-Presse, "Israel Carries Out First Gaza Arrest Raid Since Withdrawing," 24 June 2006.
8. Beirut Center for Research and Information, "Poll Finds Support for Hizbullah's Retaliation," 29 July 2006, online at http://www .beirutcenter.info/default.asp?contentid=692&MenuID=46. See also Nicholas Blanford, "Israeli Strikes May Boost Hizbullah Base," *Christian Science Monitor,* 28 July 2006.
9. Ilene R. Prusher, "Hamas Win Shatters Status Quo," *Christian Science Monitor,* 27 January 2006.
10. B'Tselem, *One Big Prison: Freedom of Movement to and from the Gaza Strip on the Eve of the Disengagement Plan,* March 2005, online at http://www.btselem.org/Download/200503_Gaza_Prison_ English.pdf.

11. See the reports of Amira Hass for *Ha'aretz* newspaper in Hebrew, reprinted selectively in the English edition and online. See, for example, Amira Hass, "Impossible Travel," *Ha'aretz*, 1 February 2007; and "The Real Disaster Is the Closure," *Ha'aretz*, 21 May 2002.

12. For details, see Stephen R. Shalom, "Lebanon War Question and Answer," ZNet, 7 August 2006, online at http://www.zmag.org/content/showarticle.cfm?ItemID=10721. See also Zeev Moaz, "The War of Double Standards," *Ha'aretz*, 20 July 2006.

13. Ayatollah Sayyid Ali Khamenei, speech, 4 June 2006, online at http://www.khamenei.ir/EN/News/detail.jsp?id=20060604A. See also Guy Dinmore, "US Allies Urge Direct Dialogue with Iran," *Financial Times* (London), 3 May 2006.

14. Edward Peck, interviewed by Amy Goodman and Juan Gonzalez, *Democracy Now!* 28 July 2006, online at http://www.democracynow.org/article.pl?sid=06/07/28/1440244.

15. For background, see Noam Chomsky, *Fateful Triangle: The United States, Israel, and the Palestinians*, rev. ed. (Cambridge, Mass.: South End Press, 1999); Robert Fisk, *Pity the Nation*, 4th ed. (New York: Nation Books, 2002).

16. Amal Saad-Ghorayeb, "People Say No," *Al-Ahram Weekly*, 3–9 August 2006, online at http://weekly.ahram.org.eg/2006/806/op33.htm.

17. Ibid.

18. Tim Llewellyn, "Into the Valley of Death," *CounterPunch*, 8 August 2006, online at http://www.counterpunch.org/llewellyn08082006.html.

19. *New York Times* staff, "U.S. Vetoes Criticism of Israel," *New York Times*, 14 July 2006. Later on John Bolton, then U.S. ambassador to the United Nations, told the BBC he was "damned proud of what we did" to block an earlier cease-fire. BBC, "Bolton Admits Lebanon Truce Block," 22 March 2007, online at http://news.bbc.co.uk/2/hi/middle_east/6479377.stm.

20. Seymour M. Hersh, "Watching Lebanon: Washington's Interests in Israel's War," *New Yorker*, 21 August 2006, p. 28.

21. Tanya Reinhart, *Israel/Palestine: How to End the War of 1948*, rev. ed. (New York: Seven Stories Press/Open Media, 2004), p. 83.

22. In 2007, Tanya Reinhart died, aged sixty-three. See Noam Chomsky, "In Memory of Tanya Reinhart," 18 March 2007, online at http://www.chomsky.info/articles/20070318.htm.

23. Uri Avnery, "What a Wonderful Israeli Plan," *Palestine Chronicle*, 9 June 2006, online at http://www.palestinechronicle.com/story-06090613735.htm.
24. Siddharth Varadarajan, "A Defeat for Israel, but Also for Justice," *Hindu* (India), 14 August 2006, online at http://www.thehindu.com/2006/08/14/stories/2006081404201100.htm.
25. Alan Dershowitz, "Lebanon Is Not a Victim," *Huffington Post*, 7 August 2006, online at http://www.huffingtonpost.com/alandershowitz/lebanon-is-not-a-victim_b_26715.html.
26. See, for example, Eugene Robinson, "It's Disproportionate . . . ," *Washington Post*, 25 July 2006.
27. Kennan quoted in Walter LaFeber, *Inevitable Revolutions: The United States in Central America*, rev. ed. (New York: W. W. Norton, 1983), pp. 109, 112.
28. Borzou Daragahi, "Iraqis Find Rare Unity in Condemning Israel," *Los Angeles Times*, 24 July 2006.
29. Edward Wong and Michael Slackman, "Iraqi Denounces Israel's Actions," *New York Times*, 20 July 2006.
30. Edward Epstein, "Iraqi Leader Addresses Congress, His Country," *San Francisco Chronicle*, 27 July 2006.
31. See, for example, Thomas L. Friedman, "Time for Plan B," *New York Times*, 4 August 2006.
32. David E. Sanger, "An Old Presidential Predicament: China Proves Tough to Influence," *New York Times*, 21 April 2006; Joseph Kahn, "In Hu's Visit to the U.S., Small Gaffes May Overshadow Small Gains," *New York Times*, 22 April 2006.
33. Agence France-Presse, "Hu Ends US Tour Marked by Lack of Accords and Embarrassment," 22 April 2006.
34. William Kristol, "It's Our War: Bush Should Go to Jerusalem—and the U.S. Should Confront Iran," *Weekly Standard*, 24 July 2006.
35. Edward Luce, "Hostage to History," *Financial Times* (London), 2 June 2006.
36. Andrew Moravcsik, "Déjà Vu All Over Again," *Newsweek International*, 15 May 2006.
37. See Michael Hirsh and Maziar Bahari, "Diplo-Dancing with Iran: Rice Makes an Offer to Tehran—with Tough Conditions," *Newsweek*, 12 June 2006, p. 32.
38. David Usborne, "Iran Must Make First Move, Bush Tells UN Meeting," *Independent* (London), 20 September 2006.

39. For details, see Noam Chomsky, *Failed States: The Abuse of Power and the Assault on Democracy* (New York: Owl Books, 2007), pp. 70–75.

40. David C. Korten, *The Great Turning: From Empire to Earth Community* (San Francisco: Berrett-Koehler Publishers, 2006).

41. Robert McNamara, "Apocalypse Soon," *Foreign Policy*, May–June 2005.

42. Andy Webb-Vidal, "Chavez Hastens Drive for Bigger Share of Oil Revenues," *Financial Times* (London), 28 April 2006; Reuters, "Venezuela Begins Drive to Certify More Oil Reserves," *Globe and Mail* (Toronto), 11 August 2006.

43. Robert H. Frank, "A Health Care Plan So Simple, Even Stephen Colbert Couldn't Simplify It," *New York Times*, 15 February 2007.

44. See Noam Chomsky, *9-11* (New York: Seven Stories, 2001).

45. Charles Forelle, James Bandler, and Mark Maremont, "Executive Pay: The 9/11 Factor," *Wall Street Journal*, 15 July 2006; Mark Maremont, Charles Forelle, and James Bandler, "Companies Say Backdating Used in Days After 9/11," *Wall Street Journal*, 7 March 2007.

46. "Operations Security Impact on Declassification Management Within the Department of Defense," 13 February 1998, produced by Booz Allen & Hamilton Inc., Linthicum, Maryland, in response to Executive Order 12958, available online at http://www .fas.org/sgp/othergov/dod_opsec.html. The document recommends a declassification strategy that includes "Diversion: List of interesting declassified material—i.e. Kennedy assassination data" and also notes that "use of the Internet could reduce the unrestrained public appetite for 'secrets' by providing good faith distraction material." See also Executive Order 12958, 17 April 1995, online at http://www.fas.org/sgp/clinton/eo12958.html.

3. LATIN AMERICA: STIRRINGS IN THE SERVANTS' QUARTERS

1. Noam Chomsky, *Hegemony or Survival: America's Quest for Global Dominance* (New York: Owl, 2004), p. 16.

2. See Noam Chomsky, *Year 501: The Conquest Continues* (Boston: South End Press, 1993), chap. 1.

3. Helene Cooper, "Iran Who? Venezuela Takes the Lead in a Battle of Anti-U.S. Sound Bites," *New York Times*, 21 September 2006.

4. Colum Lynch, "Chavez Stirs Things Up at the UN: Venezuelan

Leader Wins Cheers with Rant Against U.S.," *Washington Post*, 17 September 2005.

5. For a discussion of the millennium goals, see Chomsky, *Failed States*, p. 4.

6. Ibid., pp. 79–82, 94–95.

7. Joel Brinkley, "In Word Feud with 'Hitler,' 'Satan' Draws Line in Sand," *New York Times*, 20 May 2006; Pablo Bachelet, "Chavez Throws More Barbs at Bush: Democrats Object," *Minneapolis Star Tribune*, 22 September 2006.

8. Cooper, "Iran Who?"

9. Ewen MacAskill, "US Seen as a Bigger Threat to Peace than Iran, Worldwide Poll Suggests," *Guardian* (London), 15 June 2006.

10. Andy Webb-Vidal, "Jubilation in the Barrios as Chavez Returns in Triumph," *Financial Times* (London), 15 April 2002.

11. Guy Dinmore and Isabel Gorst, "Bush to Seal Strategic Link with Kazakh Leader," *Financial Times* (London), 29 September 2006.

12. For more discussion, see Chomsky, *Failed States*, p. 137. See polling by *Latinobarómetro*, December 2006. Danna Harman, "A Castro Ally with Oil Cash Vexes the US," *Christian Science Monitor*, 20 May 2005.

13. Richard Lapper and Hal Weitzman, "Chavez Casts a Long Anti-American Shadow Over Regional Capitals," *Financial Times* (London), 3 May 2006.

14. Ibid.

15. Thomas L. Friedman, "Fill 'Er Up with Dictators," *New York Times*, 27 September 2006.

16. Adam Thomson, "US Warns Nicaraguans Not to Back Sandinista," *Financial Times* (London), 15 September 2006.

17. For details, see *The State of Working America*, issued biannually by the Economic Policy Institute and published by Cornell University Press.

18. Randeep Ramesh, "A Tale of Two Indias," *Guardian* (London).

19. P. Sainath, "Fewer Jobs, More Buses in Wayanad," *Hindu*, 27 December 2004; Indo-Asian News Service, "New Economic Policy Hard on Farmers," Indo-Asian News Service, 29 October 2004.

20. Barbara Harriss-White, *India Working* (Cambridge: Cambridge University Press, 2003).

21. For analysis, see Chomsky, *Year 501*, chap. 7; Stephen Fidler, "Aftermath of the Bank Crisis," *Financial Times* (London), 14 March 1997.

22. Chris Flood, "Copper Hits High on Codelco Strike," *Financial Times* (London), 5 January 2006.

23. Tony Smith, "Argentina Defaults on $3 Billion I.M.F. Debt," *New York Times*, 10 September 2003; Benedict Mander, "Latin Allies Forge a Political Bond," *Financial Times* (London), 12 July 2006.

24. Chomsky, *Hegemony or Survival*, p. 139.

25. Chomsky, *Failed States*, chap. 6.

26. Program on International Policy Attitudes (PIPA), "U.S. Public Would Significantly Alter Bush Administration's Budget," media release, 7 March 2005.

27. Paul Waldman, "Elections Aren't About Issues," *Boston Globe*, 6 September 2006.

28. Mara Liasson, "Barack Obama, Still on the Rise," *All Things Considered*, National Public Radio, 8 December 2006.

29. For some recent historical data, see Center for Responsive Politics, "US House Reelection Rates, 1964–2004" (http://www.opensecrets.org/bigpicture/reelect.asp?cycle=2004); "US Senate Reelection Rates, 1964–2004" (http://www.opensecrets.org/bigpicture/reelect.asp?Cycle=2004&chamb=S); and "2006 Election Overview: Incumbent Advantage—All Candidates" (http://www.opensecrets.org/overview/incumbs.asp?cycle=2006).

30. See Richard Gott, *Hugo Chávez and the Bolivarian Revolution*, rev. ed. (New York: Verso, 2005).

31. William A. Dorman and Mansour Farhang, *The U.S. Press and Iran: Foreign Policy and the Journalism of Deference* (Berkeley: University of California Press, 1987).

32. On December 31, 1977, Carter said, "Iran, because of the great leadership of the shah, is an island of stability in one of the more troubled areas of the world" and spoke of "the respect, admiration, and love which your people give to you." See Mark Tran, "Tehran's Promise of Help Could Improve Ties with Washington," *Guardian* (London), 5 August 1989.

33. For background, see Dilip Hiro, *The Longest War: The Iran–Iraq Military Conflict*, rev. ed. (New York: Routledge, 1991).

34. Gary Milhollin testimony in *United States Export Policy Toward Iraq Prior to Iraq's Invasion of Kuwait*, Hearing Before the Committee on Banking, Housing, and Urban Affairs, U.S. Senate, 102nd Congress, 27 October 1992. See also Chomsky, *Hegemony or Survival*, pp. 111–12; Chomsky, *Failed States*, pp. 28–29.

35. Mark Clayton, "A Congressman Brings Home the Fuel—from an Unorthodox Supplier," *Christian Science Monitor*, 25 November 2005.

36. Danna Harman, "Chavez Seeks Influence with Oil Diplomacy," *Christian Science Monitor*, 25 August 2005.

37. See Marc Frank, "Eye Surgeons Bring a Ray of Hope to the Caribbean," *Financial Times*, 21 October 2005.

38. Monte Reel, "A Latin American Pipeline Dream: Regional Leaders Put Weight Behind Gas Plan," *Washington Post*, 12 February 2006.

39. William Preston Jr., Edward S. Herman, and Herbert I. Schiller, *Hope and Folly: The United States and Unesco, 1945–1985* (Minneapolis: University of Minnesota Press, 1989).

40. See Amy Goodman and David Goodman, *The Exception to the Rulers* (New York: Hyperion, 2006), pp. 181–84, 188–89.

41. Bassem Mroue, "Iraqi Government Extends Closure of Al-Jazeera's Office in Baghdad Indefinitely," Associated Press, 4 September 2004.

42. Colin Powell, news conference with Sheik Hamad bin Khalifa Thani, 3 October 2001, Washington, D.C. See also Michael Dobbs, "Qatar TV Station a Clear Channel to Middle East," *Washington Post*, 9 October 2001.

43. Jonathan Curiel, "English-Language Al-Jazeera Bets Americans Will Tune In for News," *San Francisco Chronicle*, 15 November 2006.

44. Noam Chomsky, "Latin America at the Tipping Point," *International Socialist Review* 46 (March–April 2006), pp. 10–11.

45. See additional discussion in Chomsky, *Failed States*, p. 107.

46. Patrick J. McDonnell, "Leftist Presidents Take Spotlight at Trade Summit," *Los Angeles Times*, 22 July 2006; Paulo Prada, "South American Trade Bloc Moves to Admit Venezuela," *New York Times*, 8 December 2005.

47. Benedict Mander, "Instrument of Revolution," *Financial Times* (London), 8 May 2007.

48. See the poll conducted for WorldPublicOpinion.org by the Program on International Policy Attitudes (PIPA) at the University of Maryland, "Most Iraqis Want US Troops Out Within a Year," 27 September 2006.

49. Ibid.

50. See Amy Goodman, interview with Amal Saad-Ghorayeb, *Democracy Now!*, 27 June 2006, online at http://www.democracynow.org/article.pl?sid=06/07/27/1423248. Ghorayeb reports polling in Lebanon showing that "89.5 percent believe that the U.S. was not an honest broker in this current conflict. In fact, only 8 percent of Lebanese see it as playing a balanced role."

51. Scott Peterson, "Cluster Bombs: A War's Perilous Aftermath," *Christian Science Monitor*, 7 February 2007.
52. Borzou Daragahi, "Lebanon's Coast Is Drowning in Oil," *Los Angeles Times*, 4 September 2006.
53. "Tallying Mideast Damage," *Science*, 15 September 2006.
54. "Rumsfeld's Words on Iraq: 'There Is Untidiness,'" *New York Times*, 12 April 2003; Sudarsan Raghavan "Violence Changes Fortune of Storied Baghdad Street," *Washington Post*, 18 September 2006; Omayma Abdel-Latif, "Israel's Other War: A Little Remarked Consequence of Israel's War on Lebanon Is the Destruction of Culture, *Al-Ahram Weekly*, 7–13 September 2006, online at http://weekly.ahram.org.eg/2006/811/re83.htm.

4. THE UNITED STATES VERSUS THE GOSPELS

1. Jonathan Kandell, "Augusto Pinochet, 91, Dictator Who Ruled by Terror in Chile, Dies," *New York Times*, 11 December 2006.
2. See Tim Weiner, "All the President Had to Do Was Ask," *New York Times*, 13 September 1998.
3. Ariel Dorfman, "The Half-Life of a Despot," *New York Times*, 12 December 2006.
4. See Juan Hernández Pico, "Central America's Alternative: Integration from Below," *Envío* (Managua, Nicaragua), no. 151 (February 1994), online at http://www.envio.org.ni/articulo/1746. See also Noam Chomsky, *The Culture of Terrorism* (Boston: South End Press, 1988).
5. Richard Lapper, "Day of Judgment," *Financial Times* (London), 26 November 1998.
6. Peter De Shazo, "The Valparaiso Maritime Strike of 1903 and the Development of a Revolutionary Labor Movement in Chile," *Journal of Latin American Studies* 11, no. 1 (May 1979), p. 158. See also Sergio Grez Toso, "La guerra preventiva: Santa María de Iquique. Las Razones del poder," Archivo Chile (2006), online at http://www.archivochile.com/Historia_de_Chile/sta_ma/HCHsta-ma_04.pdf.
7. "From 'Governing from Below' to Governing Right Up at the Top," *Envío* (Managua, Nicaragua), no. 304 (November 2006); online at http://www.envio.org.ni/articulo/3438.
8. Editorial, "Sandinista Revista: Daniel Ortega's Comeback in Nicaragua May Raise Eyebrows, But He Poses Little Threat to the U.S.," *Los Angeles Times*, 12 November 2006.

9. Tim Rogers, "Chavez Plays Oil Card in Nicaragua," *Christian Science Monitor*, 5 May 2006.

10. Eliza Barclay, "Energy for the Future Inspires Debate: Central America Sees Renewables as Part of Its Needs for the Longer Term," *Houston Chronicle*, 25 December 2005. The article notes, "Costa Rica has led the region in renewable energy, with 90 percent of its electricity from hydroelectric, geothermal and wind-powered generators, according to Carlos Manuel Rodriguez, Costa Rica's energy and environment minister."

11. See Oscar Olivera and Tom Lewis, ¡*Cochabamba! Water War in Bolivia* (Cambridge: South End Press, 2004).

12. Simon Romero, "Early Returns Point to a Presidential Runoff in Ecuador," *New York Times*, 16 October 2006.

13. Adam Thomson, "Fury Builds in Mexico as Defeated Side Cries Fraud," *Financial Times*, 8 July 2006.

14. Molly Moore, "Micro-Credit Pioneer Wins Peace Prize," *Washington Post*, 14 October 2006.

15. Pope Benedict XVI called Islam "evil and inhuman." Ian Fisher, "Pope Calls West Divorced from Faith, Adding a Blunt Footnote on Jihad," *New York Times*, 13 September 2006.

16. Nikolai Lanine, "We're Still Dying in Afghanistan," *Globe and Mail* (Toronto), 30 November 2006.

17. Walter Pincus, "Mueller Outlines Origin, Funding of Sept. 11 Plot," *Washington Post*, 6 June 2002.

18. Karen DeYoung, "Allies Are Cautious on 'Bush Doctrine,'" *Washington Post*, 16 October 2001.

19. See Abdul Haq, "US Bombs Are Boosting the Taliban," *Guardian* (London), 2 November 2001. Excerpted from an 11 October 2001 interview with Anatol Lieven.

20. Farhan Bokhari and John Thornhill, "Afghan Peace Assembly Call," *Financial Times* (London), 26 October 2001.

21. Pamela Constable, "In Afghan Poppy Heartland, New Crops, Growing Danger," *Washington Post*, 6 May 2006; Josh Meyer, "Pentagon Doing Little in Afghan Drug Fight," *Los Angeles Times*, 5 December 2006; Carlotta Gall, "Record Opium Crop Possible in Afghanistan, U.N. Study Predicts," *New York Times*, 6 March 2007. See also the chart "Opium Cultivation in Afghanistan," *New York Times*, 6 March 2007.

22. Amy Waldman, "Afghan Route to Prosperity: Grow Poppies," *New York Times*, 10 April 2004.

23. Michael Walzer, *Arguing About War* (New Haven: Yale University Press, 2004), p. 3.
24. Ibid., p. 200, n. 1
25. Ibid.
26. Michael Walzer, *Just and Unjust Wars: A Moral Argument with Historical Illustrations*, 4th edition (New York: Basic Books, 2006).
27. Jean Bethke Elshtain, *Just War Against Terror* (New York: Basic Books, 2003).
28. Chomsky, *Hegemony or Survival*, pp. 95, 199, 203.
29. David Zeiger, *Sir! No Sir!* (Displaced Films/Documara, 2007); David Cortright, *Soldiers in Revolt*, rev. ed. (Chicago: Haymarket Books, 2005).
30. Michelle York, "This Café's Menu Is Slight but Its Mission Ambitious," *New York Times*, 19 November 2006.
31. Vietnam Veterans Against the War, *The Winter Soldier Investigation: An Inquiry into American War Crimes* (Boston: Beacon Press, 1972).
32. David Krieger, "Why Are There Still Nuclear Weapons?" Nuclear Age Peace Foundation, 25 August 2006, online at http://www.wagingpeace.org/articles/2006/08/25_krieger_why.htm.
33. For background and discussion, see Chomsky, *Failed States*, pp. 69–78.
34. Robert Collier, "U.S. Action Pays Tribute to India's Rising Clout," *San Francisco Chronicle*, 19 November 2006.
35. Gary Milhollin, "The US-India Nuclear Pact: Bad for Security," *Current History*, no. 694 (November 2006), pp. 371–74.
36. Jehangir S. Pocha, "China and India on Verge of Nuclear Deal," *Boston Globe*, 20 November 2006; Farhan Bokhari and Jo Johnson, "US Fears China-Pakistan Nuclear Ties," *Financial Times* (London), 17 November 2006.

5. THE FRAMEWORK FOR THINKABLE THOUGHTS

1. Program on International Policy Attitudes, "A Majority of Americans Reject Military Threats in Favor of Diplomacy with Iran," 7 December 2006, online at http://www.worldpublicopinion.org.
2. James A. Baker III, Lee H. Hamilton, et al., *The Iraq Study Group Report: The Way Forward—A New Approach* (New York: Vintage Books, 2006).

3. Ibid., p. 49.

4. WorldPublicOpinion.org, "Most Iraqis Want US Troops Out Within a Year," 27 September 2006.

5. Steven Greenhouse, "Sharp Decline in Union Members in '06," *New York Times*, 26 January 2007.

6. Harley Shaiken, " The Employee Free Choice Act Would Give Organizing Power Back to Workers," *Los Angeles Times*, 17 February 2007.

7. "The Workplace: Why America Needs Unions, But Not the Kind It Has Now," *BusinessWeek*, 23 May 1994.

8. Mark Trumbull, "The Squeeze on American Pocketbooks," *Christian Science Monitor*, 3 February 2006.

9. Keith Bradsher, "Dollars to Spare in China's Trove," *New York Times*, 6 March 2007; Richard McGregor, "The Trillion Dollar Question," *Financial Times* (London), 25 September 2006.

10. Edward Wong, "Iran Is Playing a Growing Role in Iraq Economy," *New York Times*, 17 March 2007.

11. Ewen MacAskill, "US Threatens Firm Response to Iranian Meddling in Iraq," *Guardian* (London), 30 January 2007.

12. For background, see Noam Chomsky and Edward S. Herman, *After the Cataclysm: Postwar Indochina and the Reconstruction of Imperial Ideology* (Boston: South End Press, 1979), chaps. 1, 7.

13. See Noam Chomsky, "Watergate: A Skeptical View," *New York Review of Books* 20, no. 14 (20 September 1973).

14. For a detailed discussion, see Taylor Owen and Ben Kiernan, "Bombs Over Cambodia," *Walrus* (October 2006), online at http://www.walrusmagazine.ca/articles/2006.10-history-bombs-over-cambodia/.

15. Ibid.

16. Reprinted 7 December 2006 on ZNet, online at http://www.zmag.org/content/showarticle.cfm?ItemID=11571.

17. For further discussion, see Owen and Kiernan, "Bombs Over Cambodia."

18. Elizabeth Becker, "Kissinger Tapes Describe Crises, War and Stark Photos of Abuse," *New York Times*, 27 May 2004; Michael Dobbs, "Haig Said Nixon Joked of Nuking Hill," *Washington Post*, 27 May 2004.

19. Frank Rich, "The Sunshine Boys Can't Save Iraq," *New York Times*, 10 December 2006.

20. Glenn Beck, "What Will Change Iran Situation?" CNN, *Glenn Beck Show*, 23 August 2006.

21. David Maraniss, "Reagan Has a Texas-Sized Sales Job," *Washington Post*, 16 March 1986.

22. Andy Geller, "Bibi: Mad Mullahs Threaten 'Another Holocaust,'" *New York Post*, 15 November 2006.

23. For background, see Chomsky, *Failed States*, p. 16.

24. Quoted in Mark Landler and David E. Sanger, "Chief U.N. Nuclear Monitor Cites Iran Enrichment Plan," *New York Times*, 27 January 2007.

25. For details, see Chomsky, *Hegemony or Survival*, p. 25.

26. Dan Morrison, "Persian Populist Wins Arab Embrace," *Christian Science Monitor*, 21 June 2006; U.S. Newswire, "First Public Opinion Poll in Iran's Neighboring Countries Reveals Startling Findings on Possibility of Iranian Nuclear Arms," 12 June 2006.

27. Noam Chomsky, *On Power and Ideology: The Managua Lectures* (Boston: South End, 1987), p. 127.

28. Seymour Hersh reports: "The Pentagon has established covert relationships with Kurdish, Azeri, and Baluchi tribesmen, and has encouraged their efforts to undermine the regime's authority in northern and southeastern Iran." See Seymour Hersh, "The Next Act," *New Yorker*, 27 November 2006, p. 98.

29. Steve Inskeep, "A Key Critic's Problem with Jimmy Carter's Book," *Morning Edition*, NPR, 26 January 2007.

30. UN Security Council Resolution 497 (17 December 1981).

31. For discussion, see Chomsky, *Failed States*, p. 45.

32. Renée Montagne, "Longtime Jerusalem Mayor Teddy Kollek Dies at 95," *Morning Edition*, NPR, 2 January 2007.

33. For discussion, see Noam Chomsky, *World Orders Old and New*, rev. ed. (New York: Columbia University Press, 1996), pp. 287–88; and Chomsky, *Fateful Triangle*, pp. 546–47.

34. UN Security Council Resolution 252 (21 May 1968).

35. Juan Williams, interview with President George W. Bush, "President Bush on the Record, Part 1," *All Things Considered*, NPR, 29 January 2007.

36. Baker, Hamilton, et al., *The Iraq Study Group Report*, p. 74.

37. Guy Dinmore, "US Twists Civilian Arms to Fill Its Fortress Baghdad," *Financial Times* (London), 8 January 2007.

38. Quoted in Mark Steel, *Vive la Revolution: A Stand-up History of the French Revolution* (Chicago: Haymarket Books, 2006), p. 73.

39. For discussion, see Chomsky, *Hegemony or Survival*, p. 11.

40. G. John Ikenberry, "America's Imperial Ambition," *Foreign Affairs* 81, no. 5 (September–October 2002).

6. INVASIONS AND EVASIONS

1. The *Globe* ran a survey of thirty-nine major U.S. newspapers in 1968 and found that none had editorialized against the war. *Boston Globe*, 18 February 1968. Cited in Norman Solomon, *War Made Easy: How Presidents and Pundits Keep Spinning Us to Death* (Hoboken, New Jersey: John Wiley & Sons, 2007), p. 223.

2. Walter Lippmann, *Men of Destiny* (New York: Macmillan, 1927), pp. 215–16.

3. Bernard Porter, *Empire and Superempire: Britain, America and the World* (New Haven: Yale University Press, 2006), p. 64.

4. Ibid., pp. 20–21, 62–72.

5. Hannah Arendt, *The Origins of Totalitarianism*, rev. ed. (New York: Harcourt Brace Jovanovich, 1973), pp. 183–84.

6. See Noam Chomsky, *Language and Mind*, 3rd ed. (Cambridge, Mass.: Cambridge University Press, 2006), p. 10.

7. For an excellent overview, see Stephen Jay Gould, *The Mismeasure of Man*, rev. ed. (New York: W. W. Norton, 1996).

8. Paul Krugman, "Reign of Error," *New York Times*, 28 July 2006.

9. Program on International Policy Attitudes, "Three in Four Say If Iraq Did Not Have WMD or Support al Qaeda, US Should Not Have Gone to War," media release, 28 October 2004, online at http://www.pipa.org/OnlineReports/Iraq/IraqPresElect_Oct04/IraqPresElect_Oct04_pr.pdf.

10. For background, see Philip Weiss, "Too Hot for New York," *Nation*, 3 April 2006, online at http://www.thenation.com/doc/20060403/weiss.

11. John Mearsheimer and Stephen Walt, "The Israel Lobby," *London Review of Books* 28, no. 6 (23 March 2006), online at http://www.lrb.co.uk/v28/n06/mear01_.html.

12. Norman Podhoretz, *Making It* (New York: Random House, 1967).

13. Eugene Goodheart, "The London Review of Hezbollah," *Dissent*,

no. 62 (Winter 2007), online at http://www.dissentmagazine.org/article/?article=733.

14. For background and analysis, see Chomsky, *Fateful Triangle*, pp. 9–27.

15. Ibid., p. 21. See "Issues Arising Out of the Situation in the Near East," 29 July 1958, in *Foreign Relations of the United States, 1958–1960*, vol. 12, *Near East Region; Iraq; Iran; Arabian Peninsula* (Washington: U.S. Government Printing Office, 1993), pp. 114–24, esp. p. 119.

16. See Avi Shlaim, *Collusion Across the Jordan: King Abdullah, the Zionist Movement, and the Partition of Palestine* (New York: Columbia University Press, 1988), p. 388.

17. For a detailed discussion of the revision of the Kennedy record by Schlesinger and other Kennedy memoirists after the war became unpopular, see Noam Chomsky, *Rethinking Camelot: JFK, the Vietnam War, and U.S. Political Culture* (Boston: South End Press), pp. 105–25.

18. Arthur M. Schlesinger Jr., *A Thousand Days: John F. Kennedy in the White House* (Boston: Houghton Mifflin, 1965).

19. Chomsky, *Rethinking Camelot.*

20. For discussion, see Noam Chomsky, *American Power and the New Mandarins* (New York: The New Press, 2002), chap. 4.

21. For discussion, see Noam Chomsky, *Middle East Illusions* (Lanham, MD: Rowman & Littlefield Publishers, 2004), chap. 5.

22. Howard LaFranchi, "Congress Says It Sees Jerusalem as Israel's Capital," *Christian Science Monitor,* 2 October 2002.

23. See Chomsky, *Hegemony or Survival*, p. 29.

24. Ed Crooks, "Exxon Profits May Spur Critics," *Financial Times*, 1 February 2007; Andrei Postelnicu, "Exxon Highlights Investment Amid New Earnings Record," *Financial Times* (London), 28 April 2006.

25. See Sharon Wrobel, "Industrial Cooperation Spikes 500% in '06," *Jerusalem Post*, 17 April 2007.

26. Yaakov Katz, "Arms Sales to China Resume," *Jerusalem Post*, 2 March 2006.

27. John Lancaster, "Israel Halts China Arms Deal," *Washington Post*, 13 July 2000.

28. Leon V. Sigal, "The Lessons of North Korea's Test," *Current History* no. 694 (November 2006), pp. 363–64.

29. Jimmy Carter, *Palestine: Peace Not Apartheid* (New York: Simon and Schuster, 2006).

30. Henry Siegman, "Hurricane Carter," *Nation*, 22 January 2007, online at http://www.thenation.com/doc/20070122/siegman.

31. Editorial, "Jimmy Carter vs. Jimmy Carter," *Boston Globe*, 16 December 2006.

32. For background, see Chomsky, *Fateful Triangle*, chap. 9.

33. Yehoshua Porath, *Ha'aretz* (Tel Aviv), 25 June 1982, translated from the Hebrew edition.

34. Carter, *Palestine*, Appendix 7, "Israel's Response to the Roadmap, May 25, 2003," pp. 243–47.

35. See, among other examples, Patrick E. Tyler, "With Time Running Out, Bush Shifted Mideast Policy," *New York Times*, 30 June 2002.

7. THREATS

1. Elisabeth Rosenthal and Andrew C. Revkin, "Science Panel Says Global Warming Is 'Unequivocal,'" *New York Times*, 3 February 2007.

2. "'Doomsday Clock' Moves Two Minutes Closer to Midnight," *Bulletin of the Atomic Scientists*, media release, 18 January 2007, online at http://www.thebulletin.org/media-center/announcements/20070117.html.

3. George P. Shultz, William J. Perry, Henry A. Kissinger, and Sam Nunn, "A World Free of Nuclear Weapons," *Wall Street Journal*, 4 January 2007.

4. David E. Sanger and William J. Broad, "U.S. Concedes Uncertainty on Korean Uranium Effort," *New York Times*, 1 March 2007.

5. For a thorough analysis, see Mike Davis, *The Monster at Our Door: The Global Threat of Avian Flu*, rev. ed. (New York: Owl, 2006).

6. John Vidal, "Desert Cities Are Living on Borrowed Time, UN Warns," *Guardian* (London), 5 June 2006.

7. David R. Francis, "Spend Money on Disasters Before They Happen," *Christian Science Monitor*, 17 October 2005.

8. William J. Broad, "With a Push from the UN, Water Reveals Its Secrets," *New York Times*, 26 July 2005.

9. World Bank studies, online at http://econ.worldbank.org. See also David White, "Uneven Distribution," *Financial Times* (London), 21 November 2006.

10. Program on International Policy Attitudes, "23 Nation Poll Finds Strong Support for Dramatic Changes at UN," media release, 21 March 2005, online at http://www.worldpublicopinion.org.

11. Union of Concerned Scientists, *Smoke, Mirrors, and Hot Air*, January 2007, online at www.ucsusa.org/assets/documents/global_warming/exxon_report.pdf.

12. Peter Bergen and Paul Cruickshank, "The Iraq Effect," *Mother Jones*, 1 March 2007, online at http://www.motherjones.com/news/featurex/2007/03/iraq_effect_1.html.

13. The MIPT-RAND terrorism database is available online at http://terrorismknowledgebase.org.

14. Helene Cooper and Jim Yardley, "Pact with North Korea Draws Fire from a Wide Range of Critics in U.S.," *New York Times*, 14 February 2007.

15. Gordon Fairclough and Carla Anne Robbins, "North Korea Vows to Give Up Nuclear Weapons," *Wall Street Journal*, 20 September 2005.

16. Sigal, "Lessons of North Korea's Test."

17. Steven R. Weisman and Donald Greenlees, "U.S. Discusses Freeing North Korean Funds," *New York Times*, 1 March 2007. See also Anna Fifield, "North Korea Calls for Swift End to All Sanctions," *Financial Times* (London), 16 May 2007.

18. "Stammen die 'Supernotes' von der CIA?" *Frankfurter Allgemeine Zeitung*, 6 January 2007.

19. Edward Cody, "China Confirms Firing Missile to Destroy Satellite," *Washington Post*, 24 January 2007.

20. Chomsky, *Hegemony or Survival*, pp. 219–29.

21. Thomas E. Ricks and Craig Whitlock, "Putin Hits U.S. Over Unilateral Approach," *Washington Post*, 11 February 2007.

22. Gary Lee, "Gorbachev Drops Objection to United Germany in NATO," *Washington Post*, 17 July 1990.

23. Steven Lee Myers, "NATO Takes Steps to Expand Ranks into Eastern Europe," *New York Times*, 11 December 1996.

24. Peter Spiegel, "U.S. Ups Ante on Missile Defense," *Los Angeles Times*, 4 April 2007.

25. John Steinbruner and Jeffrey Lewis, "The Unsettled Legacy of the Cold War," *Daedalus*, Fall 2002, pp. 5–10.

26. Program on International Policy Attitudes, "Majority of Americans Reject Military Threats."

27. For discussion, see Chomsky, *Failed States*, pp. 73–74; and Chomsky, *Hegemony or Survival*, pp. 159–60.

28. Polling by Chicago Council on Foreign Relations and Gallup. For discussion, see Chomsky, *Rethinking Camelot*, pp. 60–63.

29. Edward S. Herman and Noam Chomsky, *Manufacturing Consent: The Political Economy of the Mass Media* (New York: Pantheon, 1988).

30. Edward S. Herman and Noam Chomsky, *Manufacturing Consent: The Political Economy of the Mass Media*, rev. ed. (New York: Pantheon, 2002), pp. xi–lviii.

31. Ibid., pp. 29–31. For criticisms of the limits of this approach, see pp. xvii–xviii.

32. See Fawaz Gerges, *The Far Enemy: Why Jihad Went Global* (Cambridge, Mass.: Cambridge University Press, 2005), and *Journey of the Jihadist: Inside Muslim Militancy* (New York: Harcourt Press, 2006). See also Gerges's articles online at http://pages.slc.edu/~fgerges/.

33. See Jason Burke, *Al-Qaeda: The True Story of Radical Islam* (London: Penguin Books, 2004).

34. Michael Scheuer, *Imperial Hubris: Why the West Is Losing the War on Terror* (Dulles, VA: Potomac Books, 2004), originally published anonymously.

35. Samuel P. Huntington, *The Clash of Civilizations and the Remaking of World Order* (New York: Simon and Schuster, 1996), p. 258.

36. David E. Sager, "Real Politics: Why Suharto Is In and Castro Is Out," *New York Times*, 31 October 1995.

37. George Orwell, *1984* (New York: Signet Classics, 2005), pp. 71–72.

8. WHAT WE CAN DO

1. Rick Atkinson and Ann Devroy, "Bush: Iraq Won't Decide Timing of Ground War," *Washington Post*, 2 February 1991. Bush proclaimed during a tour of military bases in North Carolina and Georgia, "When we win, and we will, we will have taught a dangerous dictator, and any tyrant tempted to follow in his footsteps, that the U.S. has a new credibility, and that what we say goes."

2. Wire reports, "Bush Assails 'Evil' of Hussein," *St. Petersburg Times*, 2 February 1991. Bush said in the same speech, "There is no place for lawless aggression in the Persian Gulf and in this new world

order that we seek to create. And we mean it, and he [Saddam Hussein] will understand that when the day is done."

3. Serge Schmemann, "All Aboard: America's War Train Is Leaving the Station," *New York Times*, February 2, 2003. Washington's message, Schmemann wrote, is no longer "you're either with us or against us," but "something far more shrewd": "Either you're with us, or you're irrelevant."

4. In a 1994 speech, Bolton said, "There is no United Nations. There is an international community that occasionally can be led by the only real power left in the world—that's the United States—when it suits our interests and when we can get others to go along." Quoted in editorial, "Questioning Mr. Bolton," *New York Times*, 13 April 2005.

5. For discussion, see Chomsky, *Hegemony or Survival*, pp. 4, 131–36.

6. For background, see Noam Chomsky, "Memories," *Z magazine* (July–August 1995), online at http://www.chomsky.info.

7. For background and discussion, see Noam Chomsky, *Deterring Democracy* (New York: Verso, 1991), pp. 149–73.

8. See Noam Chomsky and Edward S. Herman, *The Washington Connection and Third World Fascism* (Boston: South End Press, 1979); and Chomsky and Herman, *After the Cataclysm: Postwar Indochina and the Reconstruction of Imperial Ideology* (Boston: South End Press, 1979) (vols. 1 and 2 of *The Political Economy of Human Rights*). See also Edward S. Herman, *The Real Terror Network: Terrorism in Fact and Propaganda* (Boston: South End Press, 1982).

9. Lars Schoultz, "U.S. Foreign Policy and Human Rights Violations in Latin America: A Comparative Analysis of Foreign Aid Distributions," *Comparative Politics* 13, no. 2 (January 1981), pp. 155, 157.

10. For discussion, see Chomsky, *Hegemony or Survival*, pp. 52–53.

11. Alfredo Molano, *Dispossessed: Chronicles of the Desterrados of Colombia*, trans. Daniel Bland (Chicago: Haymarket Books, 2005), see foreword by Aviva Chomsky.

12. See C. Peter Rydell and Susan S. Everingham, *Controlling Cocaine: Supply Versus Demand Programs*, Rand Corporation (2004), online at http://www.rand.org/pubs/monograph_reports/MR331/index2.html.

13. Hugh O'Shaughnessy and Sue Branford, *Chemical Warfare in Colombia: The Costs of Coca Fumigation* (London: Latin America Bureau, 2005), p. 120, citing Martin Jelsma and Pien Metaal, "Cracks in the Vienna Consensus: The UN Drug Control Debate," *Drug*

War Monitor, Washington, D.C., Washington Office on Latin America, January 2004.

14. Ewen MacAskill and Suzanne Goldenberg, "Bush's Last Stand," *Guardian* (London), 11 January 2007; Michael Gordon, "Deadliest Bomb in Iraq Is Made in Iran, U.S. Says," *New York Times*, 10 February 2007.

15. For background, see Chomsky, *Deterring Democracy*, pp. 45–49.

16. For discussion, see Chomsky, *Failed States*, pp. 89–93.

17. Isabel Hilton, "Overdue Process," *Financial Times Weekend Magazine*, 28 August 2004, p. 16.

18. Universal Declaration of Human Rights, Article 14, Part 1, adopted 10 December 1948 by the General Assembly of the United Nations, online at http://www.un.org/Overview/rights.html.

19. Lynne Duke, "U.S. Camp for Haitians Described as Prison-Like," *Washington Post*, 19 September 1992.

20. Amy Goldstein, "Justices Won't Hear Detainee Rights Cases—for Now," *Washington Post*, 3 April 2007.

21. In early 1964, the State Department Policy Planning Council explained, "The primary danger we face in Castro is . . . in the impact the very existence of his regime has upon the leftist movement in many Latin American countries. . . . The simple fact is that Castro represents a successful defiance of the US, a negation of our whole hemispheric policy of almost a century and a half." Quoted in Piero Gleijeses, *Conflicting Missions: Havana, Washington, and Africa, 1959–1976* (Chapel Hill: University of North Carolina Press, 2003), p. 26.

22. Michael Janofsky, "As Cuba Plans Offshore Wells, Some Want U.S. to Follow Suit," *New York Times*, 9 May 2006.

23. Joseph Carroll, "Two in Three Americans Favor Re-Establishing Ties with Cuba," Gallup News Service, 15 December 2006.

24. Simon Romero, "Oilmen Meet with Cubans in Mexico, but U.S. Intervenes," *New York Times*, 4 February 2006.

25. David J. Lynch, "Political, Tech Hurdles Muddle Iran Oil Industry," *USA Today*, 14 September 2006.

26. Farah Stockman, "Iran's Nuclear Vision First Glimpsed at MIT," *Boston Globe*, 12 March 2007.

27. For discussion, see Chomsky, *Failed States*, p. 73.

28. Gareth Smyth, "Tehran to Ration Petrol and Put Up Pump Prices," *Financial Times* (London), 9 March 2007.

29. Sebnem Arsu, "Suspects in Journalist's Killing Came from a Hotbed of Turkish Ultranationalist Sentiment," *New York Times*, 8 February 2007.

30. Nicholas Birch, "Speaking Out in the Shadow of Death," *Guardian* (London), 7 April 2007.

31. Ian Fisher, "Turkish Writers Say Efforts to Stifle Speech May Backfire," *New York Times*, 6 October 2006; Lawrence Van Gelder, "Chomsky Publisher Charged in Turkey," *New York Times*, 5 July 2006.

32. Robert Fisk, "Shimon Peres Stands Accused Over Denial of 'Meaningless' Armenian Holocaust," *Independent* (London), 18 April 2001.

33. Special to the *New York Times*, "Genocide Seminar, Opposed by Israel, Opens," *New York Times*, 22 June 1982.

34. Molly Moore, "Naval Exercise Builds Mideast Ties," *Washington Post*, 14 January 2001; Scott Peterson, "Eager for Closer Israel Ties, Turkey Turns Up the Charm," *Christian Science Monitor*, 10 July 1998; Judy Dempsey, "Turkey to Boost Ties with Israel," *Financial Times* (London), 7 July 1998; Efraim Inbar, *The Israeli-Turkish Entente* (London: King's College London Mediterranean Studies, 2001).

35. For some indications, see Douglas Davis, "Israel Spies on Syria from Turkey," *Jerusalem Post*, 11 December 1997; Arieh O'Sullivan, "IAF Jets Fly Long-Range Training Sorties in Turkey," *Jerusalem Post*, 12 December 1997; Robert Olson, "Turkey-Iran Relations, 2000–2001: The Caspian, Azerbaijan, and the Kurds," *Middle East Policy* 9, no. 2 (June 2002), pp. 111–29.

36. Bryan Bender, "Pentagon Plans New Command to Cover Africa," *Boston Globe*, 21 December 2006.

37. Emily Wax, "A U.S. Beachhead on Horn of Africa: Region's Importance in War on Terror Grows with Use of Strategic Djibouti," *Washington Post*, 5 December 2002. For an example of its recent use, see Karen DeYoung, "U.S. Strike in Somalia Targets Al-Qaeda Figure," *Washington Post*, 9 January 2007.

38. See Aijaz Ahmad, "Empire Marches On," *Frontline* 24, no. 1 (13–26 January 2007), online at http://www.hinduonnet.com/fline/fl2401/.

39. Colum Lynch, "Peacekeeping Force for Somalia Approved," *Washington Post*, 7 December 2006.

40. Ahmad, "Empire Marches On."

41. Stephanie McCrummen, "Somali Capital Awash in Anger at Ethiopia, U.S., Interim Leaders," *Washington Post,* 11 January 2007.
42. Ewen MacAskill, "Stakes Rise as US Declares Darfur Killings Genocide," *Guardian* (London), 10 September 2004.
43. Mahmood Mamdani, "The Politics of Naming: Genocide, Civil War, Insurgency," *London Review of Books* 29, no. 5 (8 March 2007), online at http://www.lrb.co.uk/v29/n05/mamd01_.html.
44. Amira Hass has written extensively on the closures and checkpoints in a series of articles for *Ha'aretz,* forthcoming in expanded form from Metropolitan Books. See also chapter 2, note 11, and Amira Hass, foreword to Yehudit Kirstein Keshet, *Checkpoint Watch: Testimonies from Occupied Palestine* (London: Zed Books, 2006), pp. x–xvii.
45. For discussion, see Chomsky, *Fateful Triangle,* pp. 64–80.
46. Ibid., p. 67.
47. Noam Chomsky and Gilbert Achcar, *Perilous Power: The Middle East and U.S. Foreign Policy,* ed. Stephen Shalom (Boulder: Paradigm, 2006), p. 193.
48. See Jon Bekken, "The Working-Class Press at the Turn of the Century," in *Ruthless Criticism: New Perspectives in US Communication History,* ed. William S. Solomon and Robert W. McChesney (Minneapolis: University of Minnesota Press, 1993), pp. 157–59; and Ira Kipnis, *The American Socialist Movement, 1897–1912* (Chicago: Haymarket Books, 2004).
49. Chomsky, *Failed States,* pp. 228–30.
50. Eqbal Ahmad, "Intellectuals, Ideology, and the State," Cambridge, Massachusetts, 16 October 1998, audio and transcript available from *Alternative Radio* (http://www.alternativeradio.org).

ACKNOWLEDGMENTS

Special thanks to Sara Bershtel and Riva Hocherman of Metropolitan Books, Anthony Arnove for advice and friendship, David Peterson for tracking down articles, Elaine Bernard and Greg Gigg for their solidarity, KGNU community radio, Bev Stohl for her good cheer and assistance, and to Noam Chomsky for his endless patience and good humor. Parts of these interviews first appeared in the *International Socialist Review*.

INDEX

C

D

He just wanted a decent book to read ...

Not too much to ask, is it? It was in 1935 when Allen Lane, Managing Director of Bodley Head Publishers, stood on a platform at Exeter railway station looking for something good to read on his journey back to London. His choice was limited to popular magazines and poor-quality paperbacks – the same choice faced every day by the vast majority of readers, few of whom could afford hardbacks. Lane's disappointment and subsequent anger at the range of books generally available led him to found a company – and change the world.

'We believed in the existence in this country of a vast reading public for intelligent books at a low price, and staked everything on it'
Sir Allen Lane, 1902–1970, founder of Penguin Books

The quality paperback had arrived – and not just in bookshops. Lane was adamant that his Penguins should appear in chain stores and tobacconists, and should cost no more than a packet of cigarettes.

Reading habits (and cigarette prices) have changed since 1935, but Penguin still believes in publishing the best books for everybody to enjoy. We still believe that good design costs no more than bad design, and we still believe that quality books published passionately and responsibly make the world a better place.

So wherever you see the little bird – whether it's on a piece of prize-winning literary fiction or a celebrity autobiography, political tour de force or historical masterpiece, a serial-killer thriller, reference book, world classic or a piece of pure escapism – you can bet that it represents the very best that the genre has to offer.

Whatever you like to read – trust Penguin.